Luther's Catechisms

The Lutheran Confessions Series

Edited by Kenneth Wagener and Robert C. Baker

Unless otherwise indicated, Scripture quotations are from The Holy Bible, English Standard Version, copyright © 2001 by Crossway Bibles, a division of Good News Publishers. Used by permission. All rights reserved.

Scripture quotations from *Luther's Small Catechism with Explanation* are taken from the Holy Bible New International Version ®. NIV ®. Copyright © 1973, 1978, 1984 by International Bible Society. Used by permission of Zondervan Publishing House. All rights reserved.

Except as indicated, the quotations from the Small Catechism and the Large Catechism are from *Concordia: The Lutheran Confessions*, copyright © 2005 Concordia Publishing House. All rights reserved.

The section on the Office of the Keys in Session 12 is from *Luther's Small Catechsim with Explanation*, copyright © 1986, 1991 Concordia Publishing House.

This publication may be available in braille, in large print, or on cassette tape for the visually impaired. Please allow 8 to 12 weeks for delivery. Write to the Library for the Blind, 7550 Watson Rd., St. Louis, MO 63119-4409; call toll-free 1-888-215-2455; or visit the Web site: www.blindmission.org.

Manufactured in the United States of America

1 2 3 4 5 6 7 8 9 10   15 14 13 12 11 10 09 08 07 06

Contents

Introduction

The Story of Luther's Catechisms

In 1517 Martin Luther posted his Ninety-five Theses on the door of the Castle Church in Wittenberg. By 1528 the Evangelical churches in Saxony and other parts of Germany had achieved some sort of external stability. But because of lazy and uneducated clergy and careless and uninformed people, the conditions of the congregations were pitiful. After a visit to the congregations in the fall of 1528, during which the spiritual ignorance and need of the churches became painfully clear, Luther determined to correct this situation by the preparation of two catechisms, the Large Catechism and the Small Catechism.

Luther's concern about the careless manner in which the pastors taught their congregations was expressed in rather strong language in his preface to the Large Catechism.

> For sadly we see that many pastors and preachers are very negligent in this matter and slight both their office and this teaching. Some . . . because of great and high art . . . others . . . from sheer laziness and care for their bellies. . . .

> Oh, they are completely shameful gluttons and servants of their own bellies. They are more fit to be swineherds and dog tenders than caretakers of souls and pastors. (Concordia, p. 377)

Although both catechisms were published in 1529, they are not identical, nor is the Small Catechism a condensation of the Large Catechism. The Small Catechism was designed for individual use by pastors and laypersons alike or for use in homes for the instruction of children, while the Large Catechism was intended to assist pastors in their task of teaching the chief parts of Christian doctrine. For that reason the Large Catechism is longer, more theological, and more polemical. The content is basically a revision of Luther's own series of sermons on the chief parts of the Christian faith.

Using This Guide

Each of these study guides on the Lutheran Confessions has thirteen sessions that are divided into four easy-to-use sections.

Focus—Section 1 focuses the participant's attention on the key concept that will be discovered in the session.

Inform—Section 2 explores a portion of the Confessions and questions that help the participant study the text.

Connect—Section 3 helps the participant apply the doctrine to his or her life.

Vision—Section 4 provides the participant with practical suggestions for taking the theme of the lesson out of the classroom and into the world.

May God bless the study of His truth, as we celebrate His grace to us through Jesus, our Lord. By the power of the Holy Spirit, may we focus again on the rich heritage that is ours as the people of God in Christ.

Session 1

The Lord Alone Is God

The First Commandment and Close of the Commandments

Law/Gospel Focus

God commands us to "fear, love, and trust" Him in all life's circumstances. Because of our sinful, self-centered nature, we create our own gods and put our faith in our idols. Yet God in Christ forgives us. By the Spirit's power God brings us to cling to Christ for every blessing.

Opening Worship

Read responsively the following litany based on Psalm 46.

Leader: God is our refuge and strength, a very present help in trouble.

Participants: **Therefore we will not fear though the earth gives way, though the mountains be moved into the heart of the sea,**

Leader: Though its waters roar and foam, though the mountains quake with its swelling.

Participants: **There is a river whose streams make glad the city of God, the holy habitation of the Most High.**

Leader: God is in the midst of her, she shall not be moved; God will help her when morning dawns.

Participants: **The LORD of hosts is with us; the God of Jacob is our fortress.**

God Is . . .

Who is God? Who or what is my god? Many people today are asking these questions. Their answers, however, vary as men and women explore different religious traditions and forge their own blend of beliefs and practices.

In the catechisms, Luther answers, on the basis of the Holy Scriptures, the fundamental question, "Who is *my* God?"

1. In what ways is the renewed interest in religion and spirituality a positive factor in today's society? In what ways is it a negative?

2. What evidence of a "blended spirituality" do you see in American religions today?

3. In what ways do people look at "religion" as a do-it-yourself project?

No Other Gods

The Small Catechism

The First Commandment

You shall have no other gods.

What does this mean? We should fear, love, and trust in God above all things.

The Close of the Commandments

What does God say about all these commandments? He says: "I the LORD your God am a jealous God, visiting the iniquity of the fathers on the children to the third and fourth generation of those who hate Me, but showing steadfast love to thousands of those who love Me and keep My commandments." (Exodus 20:5–6)

What does this mean? God threatens to punish all who sin against these commandments. Therefore, we should fear His wrath and not act contrary to these commandments. But He promises grace and every blessing to all who keep these commandments. Therefore, we should also love and trust in Him and gladly do what He commands.

The Large Catechism

The First Commandment

You shall have Me alone as your God. What is the meaning of this, and how is it to be understood? What does it mean to have a god? Or, what is God?

Answer: A god means that from which we are to expect all good and in which we are to take refuge in all distress. So, to have a God is nothing other than trusting and believing Him with the heart.

. . . The confidence and faith of the heart alone make both God and an idol. If your faith and trust is right, then your god is also true. On the other hand, if your trust is false and wrong, then you do not have the true God. For these two belong together, faith and God (Hebrews 11:6). Now, I say that whatever you set your heart on and put your trust in is truly your god.

The purpose of this commandment is to require true faith and trust of the heart, which settles upon the only true God and clings to Him alone. It is like saying, "See to it that you let Me alone be your God, and never seek another." (LC I 1–4)

So you can easily understand what and how much this commandment requires. A person's entire heart and all his confidence must be placed in God alone and in no one else. (LC I 13)

For [idolatry] happens not merely by erecting an image and worshiping it, but rather it happens in the heart. For the heart stands gaping at something else. It seeks help and consolation from creatures, saints, or devils. It neither cares for God, nor looks to Him for anything better than to believe that He is willing to help. The heart does not believe that whatever good it experiences comes from God (James 1:17). (LC I 21)

The Close of the Commandments

Therefore, let everyone seriously take this passage to heart, lest it be regarded as though a man had spoken it. For you it is a question of eternal blessing, happiness, and salvation, or of eternal wrath, misery, and woe. What more would you have or desire than God so kindly promising to be yours with every blessing and to protect and help you in all need? But unfortunately, here is the failure: the world believes none of this, nor regards it as God's Word. (LC I 41–42)

Discussing the Texts

4. Describe, as completely as possible, what God commands by the following words:

Fear:

Love:

Trust:

5. Underline the words in the sections from the Small and Large Catechisms that point to God's absolute claim on His creatures.

6. What, according to Luther, does it mean to "have a god"? What does his definition reveal about our human condition?

7. List the idols that human beings make in our world today. In what ways do we "worship" these gods?

8. True faith and confidence, Luther notes, "clings" to God alone. Give examples of what it means to cling to God in life.

9. In what ways does the First Commandment address our inmost thoughts, attitudes, and concerns in life?

10. Tell how the First Commandment incorporates all other commandments.

11. Relate Jesus' life, death, and resurrection for us to the meaning of the Close of the Commandments.

This Merciful God

The Ten Commandments confront us with God's will and our failures. We have no power to place God first in our lives. We have no strength or inclination to cling to God and never seek another Lord. Yet God in His mercy redeems us from slavery to our idols through Jesus Christ. Baptized into Christ's death and resurrection, we are freed from the guilt of our idolatry and disobedience.

The Large Catechism

The First Commandment

Let the following point be made to the simple; then they may well note and remember the meaning of this commandment: We are to trust in God alone and look to Him and expect from Him nothing but good, as from one who gives us body, life, food, drink, nourishment, health, protection, peace, and all necessaries of both temporal and eternal things. He also preserves us from misfortune. And if any evil befall us, He delivers and rescues us. . . .

Let everyone, then, see to it that he values this commandment great and high above all things. Do not regard it as a joke! Ask and examine your heart diligently (2 Corinthians 13:5), and you will find out whether it clings to God alone or not. If you have a heart that can expect of Him nothing but what is good—especially in need and distress—and a heart that also renounces and forsakes everything that is not God, then you have the only true God. (LC I 24, 28)

The Close of the Commandments

But as terrible as these threatenings are, so much more powerful is the consolation in the promise. For those who cling to God alone should be sure that He will show them mercy. In other words, He will show them pure goodness and blessing, not only for themselves, but also to their children and their children's children, even to the thousandth generation and beyond that. This ought certainly to move and impel us to risk our hearts in all confidence with God (Hebrews 4:16; 10:19–23), if we wish all temporal and eternal good. For the supreme Majesty makes such outstanding offers and presents such heartfelt encouragements and such rich promises. (LC I 39–40)

12. Describe what it means to "cling," as a redeemed child of God, to Christ alone for every good.

13. Tell how God demonstrated His grace to be "more powerful" than the threats and curses of the Law?

14. In the Gospel, how does God make "such outstanding offers" and present "such heartfelt encouragements and such rich promises" in your life?

15. Look at Luther's list of blessings from God. What are you most thankful for today?

16. In your words, complete the sentences below.
To love God through Christ means

To trust God through Christ means

Fear, Love, and Trust

Personal Reflection

- Select a chapter from the Gospels or New Testament Letters. Read the text carefully for God's Law and Gospel. On a sheet of paper, write the threats and curses of the Law. Then write the Gospel promise that solves our human need and gives comfort to God's people in Christ.
- Watch the nightly news or a news-magazine program for evidence of false gods and idolatry in our world. Reflect on how the Gospel offers forgiveness for human sinfulness and strength to serve God in genuine "fear, love, and trust."
- Reflect on how God has blessed you through the lives of others who love God and live according to His commandments.

Family Connection

- Have each family member bring to the table or family room an object or picture of something important in their lives. Ask God's blessing and guidance on your stewardship of His gifts.
- Buy a houseplant or plant a tree in your yard as a symbol of God's goodness to your family. As possible, encourage each person to help to care for it. Thank God for His blessings of creation and life.
- Ask family members to look around your home for evidence that you love God.

Closing Worship

Sing or read aloud these stanzas from "Holy, Holy, Holy" (*LW* 168).

Holy, holy, holy, Lord God Almighty!
Early in the morning our song shall rise to Thee.
Holy, holy, holy, merciful and mighty!
God in three Persons, blessed Trinity!

Holy, holy, holy! Lord God Almighty!
All Thy works shall praise Thy name in earth and sky and sea.

Holy, holy, holy, merciful and mighty!
God in three Persons, blessed Trinity!

For Next Week

Read the Second and Third Commandments with explanations.

Session 2

Holy Name, Holy Word

The Second and Third Commandments

Law/Gospel Focus

God is holy. He reveals Himself in His holy name and Word. Yet we are unholy—separated from God's righteousness because of our sin. Jesus, the Holy One of God, makes us holy through His sacrifice on the cross. Through faith we offer our lives to God in praise and thanksgiving.

Opening Worship

Read responsively the following litany based on Psalm 100.

Leader: Make a joyful noise to the LORD, all the earth!

Participants: **Serve the LORD with gladness! Come into His presence with singing!**

Leader: Know that the LORD, He is God! It is He who made us, and we are His;

Participants: **We are His people, and the sheep of His pasture.**

Leader: Enter His gates with thanksgiving and His courts with praise! Give thanks to Him; bless His name!

Participants: **For the LORD is good; His steadfast love endures forever, and His faithfulness to all generations.**

Holy, What?

C. S. Lewis wrote, "How little people know who think that holiness is dull. When one meets the real thing . . . it is irresistible."

What is *holy* in today's world? In the catechisms, Luther explains the holy name and word of God.

17. What do people regard as holy in our world today? How have attitudes changed in past years?

18. How have attitudes toward Sunday—"the Lord's Day"—changed in your lifetime?

19. In what ways does contemporary culture reject or trivialize the holy?

In the Name

The Small Catechism

The Second Commandment

You shall not take the name of the Lord, your God, in vain.

What does this mean? We should fear and love God so that we may not curse, swear, use witchcraft, lie, or deceive by His name, but call upon it in every trouble, pray, praise, and give thanks.

The Third Commandment

You shall sanctify the holy day.

What does this mean? We should fear and love God so that we may not despise preaching and His Word, but hold it sacred, and gladly hear and learn it.

The Large Catechism

The Second Commandment

If someone now asks, "How do you understand the Second Commandment?" or "What is meant by taking God's name in vain, or misusing God's name?" answer briefly in this way: "It means misusing God's name when we call upon the Lord God—no matter how—in order to deceive or do wrong of any kind." Therefore, this commandment makes this point: God's name must not be appealed to falsely, or taken upon the lips, while the heart knows well enough—or should know—that the truth of the matter is different. . . .

But, to explain this in a few words, all misuse of the divine name happens first in worldly business and in matters that concern money, possessions, and honor. This applies publicly in court, in the market, or wherever else people make false oaths in God's name or pledge their souls in any matter. . . .

But the greatest abuse occurs in spiritual matters. These have to do with the conscience, when false preachers rise up and offer their lying vanities as God's Word (Jonah 2:8). (LC I 51, 53–54)

Now you understand what it means to take God's name in vain. In sum it means (a) to use His name simply for purposes of falsehood, (b) to assert in God's name something that is not true, or (c) to curse, swear, summon the devil, and, in short, to practice whatever wickedness one may. (LC I 62)

The Third Commandment

The simpleminded need to grasp a Christian meaning about what God requires in this commandment. . . . We keep [holy days] first of all for bodily causes and necessities, which nature teaches and requires. We keep them for the common people . . . [that] they may withdraw in order to rest for a day and be refreshed. Second, and most especially, on this day of rest (since we can get no other chance), we have the freedom and time to attend divine service. We come together to hear and use God's Word, and then to praise God, to sing and to pray (Colossians 3:16).

So when someone asks you, "What is meant by the commandment: You shall sanctify the holy day?" Answer like this, "To sanctify the holy day is the same as to keep it holy." "But what is meant by keeping it holy?" "Nothing else than to be occupied with holy words, works, and life." For the day needs no sanctification for itself. It has been created holy in itself. But God desires the day to be holy to you. (LC I 83–84, 87)

Discussing the Texts

20. "Be holy, for I the LORD your God am holy" (Leviticus 19:2). Describe God's holiness.

21. In what ways is God's *name* holy? What does His name represent?

22. "You shall not swear by My name falsely, and so profane the name of your God: I am the LORD" (Leviticus 19:12). How do we profane God's name in our speaking and actions
at home?

at work?

in our congregation?

23. What do God's names, revealed in Scripture, tell us about His nature and attributes?
Yahweh: I AM WHO I AM

Yahweh Sabaoth: The LORD of Hosts/Armies

El Shaddai: God Almighty or God the Mountain

El Olam: God the Eternal

El Roi: God Who Sees

El Elyon: God the Most High

24. What, according to Luther, is the most important part of "sanctify the holy day"?

25. In what ways do we *actively* sin against the Third Commandment? *passively* sin?

26. "We can sin against the Third Commandment while we sit in church." Do you agree or disagree? Explain your answer.

27. Luther identified two ways God blesses us when we keep holy days. Explain the value of each for a healthy, balanced life.

28. How do the First, Second, and Third Commandments relate to each other?

Source of Life

God's name is holy. His Word is holy, far above all human thoughts, plans, and accomplishments. Although we have no claim to holiness on our own, God shares His holiness with us freely and perfectly in His Son: "He is the source of your life in Christ Jesus, whom

God made our wisdom and our righteousness and sanctification and redemption" (1 Corinthians 1:30).

In Baptism, God places His holy name on us. In the Lord's Supper, Christ gives His holy, precious body and blood for our forgiveness and life. Through the holy Word, the Holy Spirit works to bring us to a knowledge of our sin and to the grace of God in Jesus.

The Large Catechism

The Second Commandment

Besides this you must also know how to use God's name rightly. For when He says, "You shall not take the name of the Lord, your God, in vain," He wants us to understand at the same time that His name is to be used properly. For His name has been revealed and given to us so that it may be of constant use and profit. So it is natural to conclude that since this commandment forbids using the holy name for falsehood or wickedness, we are, on the other hand, commanded to use His name for truth and for all good, like when someone takes an oath truthfully when it is needed and it is demanded (Numbers 30:2). This commandment also applies to right teaching and to calling on His name in trouble or praising and thanking Him in prosperity, and so on. All of this is summed up and commanded in Psalm 50:15, "Call upon Me in the day of trouble; I will deliver you, and you shall glorify Me." For all this is bringing God's name into the service of truth and using it in a blessed way. In this way His name is hallowed, as we pray in the Lord's Prayer (Matthew 6:9). (LC I 63–64)

It is also useful that we form the habit of daily commending ourselves to God (Psalm 31:5), with soul and body, wife, children, servants, and all that we have, against every need that may arise. (LC I 73)

The Third Commandment

Indeed, we Christians ought always to keep such a holy day and be occupied with nothing but holy things. This means we should daily be engaged with God's Word and carry it in our hearts and upon our lips (Psalm 119:11–13). But as said above, since we do not always have free time, we must devote several hours a week for the sake of the young, or at least a day for the sake of the entire multitude, to being concerned about this alone. We must especially teach the use of the Ten Commandments, the Creed, and the

Lord's Prayer, and so direct our whole life and being according to God's Word. At whatever time, then, this is being observed and practiced, there a true *holy day* is being kept. (LC I 89–90)

Know, therefore, that you must be concerned not only about hearing, but also about learning and retaining God's Word in memory. Do not think that this is optional for you or of no great importance. Think that it is God's commandment, who will require an account from you (Romans 14:12) about how you have heard, learned, and honored His Word. (LC I 98)

29. What "use and profit" is God's name in your life?

30. How, according to Luther, can we use God's name properly as His redeemed children? What is our motive for using God's name?

31. As our Savior High Priest, Jesus still calls on the Father for us. What does He pray? In what ways is this assurance a great comfort in our hardships?

32. St. Paul writes, "You have received the Spirit of adoption as sons, by whom we cry, 'Abba! Father!'" (Romans 8:15). Describe what it means to call on God in such a tender and intimate way.

33. How can you daily "commend" yourself—and family—to God? What will you ask?

34. List specific ways you can "remember the Sabbath" amidst all the conflicting signals in our world.

35. How does the regular reading and study of God's Word motivate you to seek His will and keep His commandments?

Study to Show Yourself

Personal Reflection

- For your Bible reading this week, reflect on God's name revealed in the Psalms. Skim three or four psalms; note the various names and titles of God. Write or speak a prayer using the different names of the Savior God.
- Prepare for weekend worship by studying the Scripture readings before the service. Or save your bulletin and review the readings during the week.
- Review the names, colors, and themes of the church year seasons. Reflect on how the different seasons relate to the life of Christ and the mission of the Church. (The front of your congregation's hymnal may have a helpful guide, or ask your pastor for resources.)

Family Connection

- Print God's name—Father, Son, and Holy Spirit—on various sheets of colored paper. Have family members write a brief prayer of thanksgiving or request on each sheet. Use the ideas during your family prayer time.
- Skim the Psalms to find ten names and titles for God (e.g., Rock, Fortress, Refuge, Tower, Savior, Lord, etc.). Write each of the ten words on a note card. Distribute cards to family members, and ask each person to give clues or act out the word. Whoever guesses correctly acts out the next note card.
- Discuss your pastor's sermon. Ask, What did God speak to our family through His Law? How did the Gospel bring us comfort?

Closing Worship

Sing or read aloud these stanzas from "Holy God, We Praise Your Name" (*LW* 171).

Holy God, we praise Your name;
Lord of all, we bow before You.

All on earth Your scepter claim;
All in heav'n above adore You.
Infinite Your vast domain,
Everlasting is Your reign.

Holy Father, holy Son,
Holy Spirit, three we name You,
Though in essence only one;
Undivided God we claim You
And, adoring, bend the knee
While we own the mystery.

For Next Week

Read the Fourth, Fifth, and Sixth Commandments with explanations.

Session 3

Authority and Absolutes

The Fourth, Fifth, and Sixth Commandments

Law/Gospel Focus

Through His Word God reveals His will for family, society, and marriage. Because of our fallen nature, we rebel against His authority and reject His absolutes. In His perfect obedience—even to death on a cross!—Jesus reconciles us to the heavenly Father. In Christ, we have forgiveness and strength to live as His people.

Opening Worship

Read responsively the following litany based on Psalm 103.

Leader: Bless the LORD, O my soul, and all that is within me, bless His holy name!

Participants: **Bless the LORD, O my soul, and forget not all His benefits,**

Leader: Who forgives all your iniquities, who heals all your diseases,

Participants: **Who redeems your life from the pit, who crowns you with steadfast love and mercy,**

Leader: Who satisfies you with good

Participants: **So that your youth is renewed like the eagle's.**

It's All Relative?

"It's not my place to say anything," Maria thought to herself. "Who am I to say what is right and wrong for others?"

For years she had worried about her neighborhood. The signs of decline were everywhere: children without supervision, parents without responsibility, couples who lived together without any sense of commitment and accountability.

"Our world seems to have no structure, no boundaries," she sighed.

Without authority in life, the walls break down quickly. In his catechisms, Luther explores the meaning of God's Word for families, life, and marriage.

36. Describe common attitudes toward authority.

37. Who and what shape our views of authority? List people and institutions with authority in our world.

38. What "absolutes" exist in our world today? What absolutes seem to have disappeared?

39. The word *boundary* comes from the root "to bind." In what ways do boundaries—in relationships, homes, and communities—bind people together? How do boundaries contribute to good order in our world?

Respect for Others

The Small Catechism

The Fourth Commandment

You shall honor your father and your mother that it may be well with you and you may live long upon the earth.

What does this mean? We should fear and love God so that we may not despise or anger our parents and masters, but give them honor, serve them, obey them, and hold them in love and esteem.

The Fifth Commandment

You shall not murder.

What does this mean? We should fear and love God so that we may not hurt or harm our neighbor in his body, but help and befriend him in every bodily need [in every need and danger of life and body].

The Sixth Commandment

You shall not commit adultery.

What does this mean? We should fear and love God so that we may lead a pure and decent life in words and deeds, and each love and honor his spouse.

The Large Catechism

The Fourth Commandment

To the position of fatherhood and motherhood God has given special distinction above all positions that are beneath it: He does not simply command us to love our parents, but to honor them. . . . In this way He separates and distinguishes father and mother from all other persons upon earth and places them at His side. For it is a far higher thing to honor someone than to love someone, because honor includes not only love, but also modesty, humility, and submission. . . . Honor requires not only that parents be addressed kindly and with reverence, but also that, both in the heart and with the body, we demonstrate that we value them very highly, and that, next to God, we regard them as the very highest. For someone we honor from the heart we must also truly regard as high and great.

We must, therefore, impress this truth upon the young (Deuteronomy 6:7) that they should think of their parents as standing in God's place. They should remember that however lowly, poor, frail, and strange their parents may be, nevertheless, they are the father and the mother given to them by God. (LC I 105–8)

The Fifth Commandment

Now, this commandment is easy enough and has often been presented, because we hear it each year in the Gospel of St. Matthew 5:20–26, where Christ Himself explains and sums it up. He says that we must not kill, neither with hand, heart, mouth, signs, gestures, help, nor counsel. Therefore, this commandment forbids everyone to be angry, except those (as we said) who are in the place of God, that is, parents and the government. For it is proper for God and for everyone who is in a divine estate to be angry, to rebuke, and to punish because of those very persons who transgress this and the other commandments (Romans 13:4).

The cause and need of this commandment is that God well knows that the world is evil (Galatians 1:4), and that this life has much unhappiness. Therefore, He has set up this and the other commandments between the good people and the evil. . . .

And briefly, He would in this way protect, set free, and keep in peace everyone against the crime and violence of everyone else. He would have this commandment placed as a wall, fortress, and refuge around our neighbor so that we do not hurt or harm him in his body.

The commandment has this goal, that no one would offend his neighbor because of any evil deed, even though he has fully deserved it. For where murder is forbidden, all cause from which murder may spring is also forbidden. (LC I 182–83, 185–86)

The Sixth Commandment

Therefore, this commandment is directed against all kinds of unchastity, whatever it may be called. Not only is the outward act of adultery forbidden, but also every kind of cause, motive, and means of adultery. Then the heart, the lips, and the whole body may be chaste and offer no opportunity, help, or persuasion toward unchastity. Not only this, but we must also resist temptation, offer protection, and rescue honor wherever there is danger and need. We must give help and counsel, so as to maintain our neighbor's honor. For whenever you abandon this effort when you could resist unchastity, or whenever you overlook it as if it did not concern you, you are as truly guilty of adultery as the one doing the deed. To speak in the briefest way, this much is required of you: everyone must live chastely himself and help his neighbor do the same. So by this commandment God wishes to build a hedge round about (Job 1:10) and protect every spouse so that no one trespasses against him or her. (LC I 202–5)

First, understand and mark well how gloriously God honors and praises this estate. For by His commandment He both approves and guards it. He has approved it above in the Fourth Commandment, "Honor your father and your mother." But here He has (as we said) hedged it about and protected it. Therefore, He also wishes us to honor it (Hebrews 13:4) and to maintain and govern it as a divine and blessed estate because, in the first place, He has instituted it before all others. He created man and woman separately, as is clear (Genesis 1:27). This was not for lewdness, but so that they might live together in marriage, be fruitful, bear children, and nourish and train them to honor God (Genesis 1:28; Psalm 128; Proverbs 22:6; Ephesians 6:4).

Therefore, God has also most richly blessed this estate above all others. In addition, He has bestowed on it and wrapped up in it everything in the world, so that this estate might be well and richly provided for. Married life is, therefore, no joke or presumption. It is an excellent thing and a matter of divine seriousness. For marriage has the highest importance to God so that people are raised up who may serve the world and promote the knowledge of God, godly living, and all virtues, to fight against wickedness and the devil. (LC I 206–8)

Discussing the Texts

40. In what ways, according to God's purposes, is parenthood distinguished "above all positions that are beneath it"?

41. How does Luther understand the word *honor*? What additional words help to describe honor? How does honor go beyond love?

42. What does it mean to be a representative? How are parents God's representatives in their family?

43. In what ways does modern life undermine authority in the family?

44. List attitudes and actions that God forbids in the Fifth Commandment.

.

45. List attitudes and actions that God desires in the Fifth Commandment.

46. What qualities and behaviors illustrate a chaste—sexually pure and decent—life?

47. List our obligations, as Luther notes, toward sexuality.

48. In what ways has marriage lost its status as a "blessed" and "excellent" institution in today's world? What benefits does God bring to society through marriage?

Like a Symphony

As an orchestra prepares for a concert, the concertmaster plays a clear and steady A. The note is both an absolute and authority: it never changes and all the instruments tune to it.

God reveals His absolutes and authority in His Word. No human being, however, can live up to His standard. Only Christ, true God and true man, has fulfilled the demands of God's Word. In His perfect obedience to His heavenly Father, Jesus demonstrates His love—love that led Him to Calvary as a sacrifice for the sins of the world. His life, death, and resurrection have brought us reconciliation with God. In Christ, we are set free from the curse of the Law to serve our Savior God.

The Large Catechism

The Fourth Commandment

For all authority flows and is born from the authority of parents. (LC I 141)

Through [civil government], as through our parents, God gives to us food, house and home, protection, and security. They bear such name and title with all honor as their highest dignity that it is our duty to honor them and to value them greatly as the dearest treasure and the most precious jewel upon earth. (LC I 150)

For those who want to be Christians are obliged in God's sight to think them worthy of double honor who minister to their souls (1 Timothy 5:17–18). They are obligated to deal well with them and provide for them. (LC I 161)

But those who keep God's will and commandment in sight have this promise: everything they give to temporal and spiritual fathers, and whatever they do to honor them, shall be richly repaid to them. They will not have bread, clothing, and money for a year or two, but will have long life, support, and peace. They shall be eternally rich and blessed. (LC I 164–65).

The Fifth Commandment

Here again we have God's Word, by which He would encourage and teach us to do true, noble, and grand works such as gentleness, patience, and, in short, love and kindness to our enemies (Galatians 5:22–23). He would ever remind us to reflect upon the First Commandment—He is our God, which means He will help, assist, and protect us in order that He may quench the desire of revenge in us.

We ought to practice and teach this; then we would have our hands full by doing good works. (LC I 195–96)

The Sixth Commandment

Let me now say in conclusion what this commandment demands: Everyone should live chaste in thought, word, and deed in his condition—that is, especially in the estate of marriage. But also everyone should love and value the spouse God gave to him (Ephesians 5:33). For where marital chastity is to be maintained, man and wife must by all means live together in love and harmony.

Then one may cherish the other from the heart and with complete faithfulness. (LC I 219)

49. How does Luther extend the concept of authority beyond the family? In what ways is this a blessing to you? to the Church? to the world?

50. In what specific ways can you honor your parents as God's gifts? your governmental leaders? your spiritual leaders?

51. What positive guidance for Christian living does Luther recognize in the Fifth Commandment? Explain how these gifts flow from the God who richly gives His gifts.

52. List ways that God's people witness to the God-given dignity and worth of all life.

53. In what ways do married couples use the gift of sexuality to honor God? In what ways do single men and women also honor God in regard to their sexuality?

To Serve and to Protect

Personal Reflection

- Write a note to a local, state, or national leader you admire. If possible, share your gratitude. Tell the leader that you are praying for him or her.

- Visit a government site on the Internet. Reflect on how the agency is part of God's authority in the world.
- Read the Song of Songs by Solomon. Highlight in your Bible the ways that God affirms marriage and love.

Family Connection

- On a note card or piece of paper, write a list of each family member's responsibilities in the home. Share how, by God's grace, these responsibilities provide order and stability in your family.
- Go grocery shopping together. Buy foods that promote good health. Purchase extra canned goods and nonperishables for your church or community food bank.
- Plan a "Family Appreciation" event. A week ahead of the event, draw names of family members from a hat (one name per person). Keep the names a secret. (Parents can help younger children.) Each person decides on a special activity or gift to express his or her love toward the family member.

Closing Worship

Sing or read aloud the stanzas from "Lord, Dismiss Us with Your Blessing" (*LW* 218).

> Lord, dismiss us with Your blessing,
> Fill our hearts with joy and peace;
> Let us each, Your love possessing,
> Triumph in redeeming grace.
> Oh, refresh us; oh, refresh us,
> Trav'ling through this wilderness.
>
> Savior, when Your love shall call us
> From our struggling pilgrim way,
> Let not fear of death appall us,
> Glad Your summons to obey.
> May we ever, may we ever
> Reign with You in endless day.

For Next Week

Read the Seventh, Eighth, Ninth, and Tenth Commandments with explanations.

Session 4

Honesty, Truth, and Integrity

The Seventh, Eighth, Ninth, and Tenth Commandments

Law/Gospel Focus

God commands us to respect and protect everything that belongs to our neighbor. Because of sin, we steal, we hurt people with our words, and we covet what God has given to others. Yet in Jesus' sacrifice, God forgives us. Our heavenly Father strengthens us to live honestly, truthfully, and with integrity through Christ.

Opening Worship

Read responsively the following litany based on Psalm 71.

Leader: In You, O LORD, I take refuge; let me never be put to shame!

Participants: **In Your righteousness deliver me and rescue me; incline Your ear to me, and save me!**

Leader: Be to me a rock of refuge, to which I may continually come;

Participants: **You have given the command to save me, for You are my rock and my fortress.**

Leader: For You, O Lord, are my hope, my trust, O LORD, from my youth.

Participants: **My mouth is filled with Your praise, and with Your glory all the day.**

Out of the Shadows

In October 1994, the U.S. Secret Service reported the arrest of a computer hacker named "Knightshadow." While working as an engineer for a long-distance company, Knightshadow wrote a software program that diverted and stored calling card numbers. More than one hundred thousand card numbers were pirated and sold to computer hackers in the U.S., who then sold the numbers to people overseas. The total cost to the company in "free" calls: $50 million.

In his catechisms, Luther examines God's will for living in the world honestly, truthfully, and with contentment.

54. In what ways have you witnessed a decline in honesty, truthfulness, and integrity in today's world? How does this affect society?

55. Do you think theft, false testimony, and greed are more common and easy today than one hundred years ago? Explain your response.

56. Explain why you agree or disagree with each of these statements:

The surest way to remain poor is to be an honest person. (Napoleon)

No legacy is so rich as honesty. (Shakespeare, *All's Well That Ends Well*)

Help Your Neighbor

The Small Catechism

The Seventh Commandment

You shall not steal.

What does this mean? We should fear and love God so that we may not take our neighbor's money or property, nor get them with bad products or deals, but help him to improve and protect his property and business.

The Eighth Commandment

You shall not bear false witness against your neighbor.

What does this mean? We should fear and love God so that we may not deceitfully belie, betray, slander, or defame our neighbor, but defend him, think and speak well of him, and put the best construction on everything.

The Ninth Commandment

You shall not covet your neighbor's house.

What does this mean? We should fear and love God so that we may not craftily seek to get our neighbor's inheritance or house, or obtain it by a show of justice and right, or any other means, but help and be of service to him in keeping it.

The Tenth Commandment

You shall not covet your neighbor's wife, or his manservant, or his maidservant, or his cattle, or anything that is his.

What does this mean? We should fear and love God so that we may not turn, force, or entice away our neighbor's wife, servants, or cattle, but urge them to stay and carefully do their duty.

The Large Catechism

The Seventh Commandment

[God] has commanded that no one shall take away from, or diminish, his neighbor's possessions. For to steal is nothing else than to get possession of another's property wrongfully. Briefly, this includes all kinds of advantage in all sorts of trade to the disadvantage of our neighbor. . . .

Therefore, let everyone know his duty, at the risk of God's displeasure: he must do no harm to his neighbor nor deprive him of profit nor commit any act of unfaithfulness or hatred in any bargain or trade. But he must also faithfully preserve his property for him, secure and promote his advantage. This is especially true when one accepts money, wages, and one's livelihood for such service. (LC I 223–24, 233)

The Eighth Commandment

Therefore, God does not want the reputation, good name, and upright character of our neighbor to be taken away or diminished, just as with his money and possessions. He wants everyone to stand in his integrity before wife, children, servants, and neighbors. In the first place, we must consider the plainest meaning of this commandment, according to the words "You shall not bear false witness." This applies to the public courts of justice, where a poor, innocent man is accused and oppressed by false witnesses in order to be punished in his body, property, or honor. . . .

Therefore, this commandment is given in the first place so that everyone shall help his neighbor to secure his rights. . . .

Next, this commandment extends very much further, if we are to apply it to spiritual jurisdiction or administration. Here it is a common occurrence that everyone bears false witness against his neighbor. . . .

In the third place, which concerns us all, this commandment forbids all sins of the tongue (James 3), by which we may injure or confront our neighbor. (LC I 256–57, 260, 262–63)

The Ninth and Tenth Commandments

Therefore, God has added these two commandments in order that it be considered sinful and forbidden to desire or in any way to aim at getting our neighbor's wife or possessions.

. . . here it is also forbidden for you to alienate anything from your neighbor, even though you could do so with honor in the eyes of the world, so that no one could accuse or blame you as though you had gotten it wrongfully.

. . . we must know that God does not want you to deprive your neighbor of anything that belongs to him, so that he suffer the loss and you gratify your greed with it. This is true even if you could keep it honorably before the world. (LC I 293, 296, 307)

Discussing the Texts

57. How does Luther define stealing? Describe some modern-day thefts that Luther never imagined.

58. What applications of the Seventh Commandment can you make to
  •   employees and employers?

- sellers and buyers?

- neighbors?

- family members?

59. According to Luther, what positive obligations toward money and possessions does God expect of all people?

60. Describe how reputation, honor, and character are valuable assets in our world.

61. In what ways does false testimony undermine justice? How does false testimony injure and destroy relationships?

62. An ancient proverb notes, "Covetousness has for its mother unlawful desire, for its daughter injustice, and for its friend violence." Explain.

63. What forces in our world today work against contentment?

64. How are the Ninth and Tenth Commandments related to the First Commandment?

Personally Speaking

For many people, law is an abstract concept—rules, regulations, and requirements written long ago, remote from everyday life. God's Law, however, is personal: "*You* shall not steal. . . . *You* shall not bear false witness." God speaks to human beings individually and calls us to answer for our thoughts, words, and actions.

Our only response is *guilty*: "I have stolen . . . slandered my neighbor . . . coveted what is not mine." We acknowledge before the righteous God, "I have broken all of Your commandments, and I cannot redeem myself." In Christ, God removes our sin; He places our guilt and shame on His Son. Jesus shouldered our failures to obey God's Word, and He died a sacrificial death for our forgiveness, life, and salvation.

The Large Catechism

The Seventh Commandment

Briefly, in summary (as in the former commandments) this is what is forbidden: (a) To do our neighbor any injury or wrong (in any conceivable manner, by impeding, hindering, and withholding his possessions and property), or even to consent or allow such injury. Instead, we should interfere and prevent it. (b) It is commanded that we advance and improve his possessions. When they suffer lack, we should help, share, and lend both to friends and foes (Matthew 5:42).

Whoever now seeks and desires good works will find here more than enough to do that are heartily acceptable and pleasing to God. In addition, they are favored and crowned with excellent blessings. So we are to be richly compensated for all that we do for our neighbor's good and from friendship. King Solomon also teaches this in Proverbs 19:17, "Whoever is generous to the poor lends to the LORD, and He will repay him for his deed." Here, then, you have a rich Lord. He is certainly enough for you. He will not allow you to come up short in anything or to lack (Psalm 37:25). (LC I 250–53)

The Eighth Commandment

Now we have the sum and general understanding of this commandment: Let no one do any harm to his neighbor with the tongue, whether friend or foe. Do not speak evil of him, no matter whether it is true or false, unless it is done by commandment or for his reformation. Let everyone use his tongue and make it serve for the best of everyone else, to cover up his neighbor's sins and infirmities (1 Peter 4:8), excuse them, conceal and garnish them with his own reputation. The chief reason for this should be the one that Christ declares in the Gospel, where He includes all commandments about our neighbor, "whatever you wish that others would do to you, do also to them" (Matthew 7:12). (LC I 285–86)

The Ninth and Tenth Commandments

Therefore, we allow these commandments to remain in their ordinary meaning. It is commanded, first, that we do not desire our neighbor's harm, nor even assist, nor give opportunity for it. But we must gladly wish and leave him what he has. Also, we must advance and preserve for him what may be for his profit and service, just as we wish to be treated (Matthew 7:12). So these commandments are especially directed against envy and miserable greed. God wants to remove all causes and sources from which arises everything by which we harm our neighbor. Therefore, He expresses it in plain words, "You shall not covet," and so on. For He especially wants us to have a pure heart (Matthew 5:8), although we will never attain to that as long as we live here. (LC I 309–10)

65. As God's redeemed child in Christ, what is your relationship to your money? your possessions and property?

66. How does the Gospel re-create and shape our attitudes toward other people—especially those in need?

67. List, as completely as possible, the purposes for which God gives us material blessings.

68. How can you, as you interact with friends and co-workers, "put the best construction on everything"? How will our families, workplaces,

and congregations be blessed as God's people "put the best construction on everything"?

69. Describe ways that you can "help and be of service" to others in your community.

70. Where does God desire His people to look for—and find—contentment?

To the Least of These

Personal Reflection

- Clean out a closet or your basement/storage area. Donate usable items and clothing to a church or Christian agency.
- Look for opportunities to encourage and affirm friends during the week. By God's power in Christ, speak words that share the Gospel of love and forgiveness.
- Use the word *contentment* as a prayer acrostic. Write out a sentence with your requests and thanksgivings.

Family Connection

- Clean out your child's or children's toys. Donate good, usable items to your church's nursery or to a community shelter.
- Volunteer as a family at a local shelter for the homeless.
- Do a family "clean sweep" around your neighborhood or community. Look for ways to clean up trash and debris and, in general, to "improve and protect" the environment.

Closing Worship

Sing or read aloud the stanzas from "Lord of Glory, You Have Bought Us" (*LW* 402).

Lord of glory, You have bought us
With Your life-blood as the price,
Never grudging for the lost ones
That tremendous sacrifice;
And with that have freely given
Blessings countless as the sand
To th'unthankful and the evil
With Your own unsparing hand.

Grant us hearts, dear Lord, to give You
Gladly, freely of Your own.
With the sunshine of Your goodness
Melt our thankless hearts of stone
Till our cold and selfish natures
Warmed by You, at length believe
That more happy and more blessed
'Tis to give than to receive.

For Next Week

Read the First Article with Luther's explanation.

Session 5

God the Father—Maker, Provider, Defender

The First Article

Law/Gospel Focus

God, the Maker of the universe, has revealed His love and mercy toward His creation in His many good gifts. Because of sin, we spoil the earth, injure one another, and reject God's will and purposes for our lives. Only in Christ does God renew and restore His people to life "abundantly" (John 10:10). As a compassionate Father, He provides for and defends us throughout our life. Forgiven and strengthened by His love, we "thank Him, praise Him, serve Him, and obey Him."

Opening Worship

Read responsively the following litany based on Psalm 98.

Leader: Oh sing to the LORD a new song, for He has done marvelous things!

Participants: **His right hand and His holy arm have worked salvation for Him.**

Leader: The LORD has made known His salvation; he has revealed His righteousness in the sight of the nations.

Participants: **He has remembered His steadfast love and faithfulness to the house of Israel. All the ends of the earth have seen the salvation of our God.**

Leader: Make a joyful noise to the Lord, all the earth;

Participants: **Make a joyful noise before the King, the LORD.**

Who's at the Center?

Worldview: 1. a conception . . . of the purpose of the world as a whole 2. philosophy of life (*Webster's Third New International Dictionary*)

In simple language, a worldview asks, "Who is at the center—the center of the universe, of history, of my life?"

In his catechisms, Luther presents the worldview shaped by the revelation of the triune God.

71. What worldview is implied by each of the symbols?

72. Contrast the two worldviews in terms of
- the natural world

- relationships

- the value of life

- the future

73. What other types of worldview do people have or make in life?

Divinely Made

The Small Catechism

The First Article

I believe in God, the Father Almighty, maker of heaven and earth.

What does this mean? I believe that God has made me and all creatures. He has given me my body and soul, eyes, ears, and all my limbs, my reason, and all my senses, and still preserves them.

In addition, He has given me clothing and shoes, meat and drink, house and home, wife and children, fields, cattle, and all my goods. He provides me richly and daily with all that I need to support this body and life.

He protects me from all danger and guards me and preserves me from all evil.

He does all this out of pure, fatherly, divine goodness and mercy, without any merit or worthiness in me. For all this I ought to thank Him, praise Him, serve Him, and obey Him.

This is most certainly true.

The Large Catechism

What do you mean by these words, "I believe in God the Father Almighty, maker of heaven and earth"? Answer: "This is what I mean and believe, that I am God's creature (2 Corinthians 5:17). I mean that He has given and constantly preserves (Psalm 36:6) for me my body, soul, and life, my members great and small, all my senses, reason, and understanding, and so on. He gives me food and drink, clothing and support, wife and children, domestic servants, house and home, and more. Besides, He causes all created things to serve for the uses and necessities of life. These include the sun, moon, and stars in the heavens, day and night, air, fire, water, earth, and whatever it bears and produces. They include birds and fish, beasts, grain, and all kinds of produce (Psalm 104). They also include whatever else there is for bodily and temporal goods, like good government, peace, and security." So we learn from this article that none of us owns for himself, nor can preserve, his life nor anything that is here listed or can be listed. This is true no matter how small and unimportant a thing it might be. . . .

Further, we also confess that God the Father has not only given us all that we have and see before our eyes, but He daily preserves and defends us against all evil and misfortune (Psalm 5:11). He directs all sorts of danger and disaster away from us. We confess that He does all this out of pure love and goodness, without our merit, as a kind Father. He cares for us so that no evil falls upon us. . . .

Now, all that we have, and whatever else is in heaven and upon the earth, is daily given, preserved, and kept for us by God. Therefore, it is clearly suggested and concluded that it is our duty to love, praise, and thank Him for these things without ceasing (1 Thessalonians 5:17–18). In short, we should serve Him with all these things, as He demands and has taught in the Ten Commandments. (LC II 13–19)

Discussing the Texts

74. Summarize God's creative and providential power according to Luther's explanation.

75. Circle or underline the personal pronouns "I," "me," and "my" that Luther used. Why do you suppose Luther wrote these explanations in the first person?

76. Describe God's motive for making, providing for, and defending His creation.

77. How does Luther recognize his position and status as a creature before God?

78. In what ways does God's creative activity continue today?

79. How does Luther's explanation exclude all boasting of our human ability and achievement?

80. Why, do you suppose, is all life—even the details—sacred to God?

81. In what ways is Luther's explanation a commentary on Psalm 139:13–17? Psalm 104?

82. What evidence of God's creative work have you been especially appreciative of lately?

Thy Word Is Truth

Who or what shapes our worldview?

Michael L. McCoy has written in *Creation Vs. Evolution* (CPH, 1996, pp. 17–18), "A person's worldview determines a set of beliefs (doctrines) which radiates out into values, actions, and possessions. Whoever or whatever is at the center of a person's worldview will determine what is true. For the Christian, the Lord God is at the center, and His Word, the Bible, determines what is true. These truths about God, man, sin, Jesus, atonement, and other teachings are beliefs that influence what is valuable and important to the Christian."

At the center is the work of the triune God—the Father who rescued His fallen creation, the Son who offered His life as a sacrifice for the sins of the world, and the Spirit who brings us to faith in the Lord and Savior Jesus Christ. In all three articles, the Apostles' Creed forges a worldview for all who call upon God, our Maker, Redeemer, and Sanctifier.

The Large Catechism

We could say much here, if we were to wander, about how few people believe this article. For we all pass over it, hear it, and say it. Yet we do not see or consider what the words teach us. For if we believed this teaching with the heart, we would also act according to it (James 2:14). We would not strut about proudly, act defiantly, and boast as though we had life, riches, power, honor, and such, of ourselves (James 4:13–16). We would not act as though others must fear and serve us, as is the practice of the wretched, perverse world. The world is drowned in blindness and abuses all the good things and God's gifts only for its own pride, greed, lust, and luxury. It never once thinks about God, so as to thank Him or acknowledge Him as Lord and Creator.

We ought, therefore, daily to recite this article. We ought to impress it upon our mind and remember it by all that meets our eyes and by all good that falls to us. Wherever we escape from disaster or danger, we ought to remember that it is God who gives and does all these things. In these escapes we sense and see His fatherly heart and His surpassing love toward us (Exodus 34:6). In this way the heart would be warmed and kindled to be thankful, and to use all such good things to honor and praise God.

We have most briefly presented the meaning of this article. This is how much is necessary at first for the most simple to learn about what we have, what we receive from God, and what we owe in return. This is a most excellent knowledge but a far greater treasure. For here we see how the Father has given Himself to us, together with all creatures, and has most richly provided for us in this life. We see that He has overwhelmed us with unspeakable, eternal treasures by His Son and the Holy Spirit, as we shall hear (Colossians 2:2). (LC II 20–21, 23–24)

83. How does the Apostles' Creed "provide" the answers in your worldview?

84. Describe God's "fatherly heart and His surpassing love."

85. Of what, according to Luther, should our blessings remind us?

86. What attitudes and behaviors characterize a worldview centered in the grace and goodness of God?

Attitude of Gratitude

Personal Reflection

• Begin or resume a regular practice of recycling in your house. If possible, check with local recycling centers for opportunities to volunteer your time and energy.

• Ask your pastor or church trustees to suggest projects that you can start or finish at your congregation. Ask a friend or group of friends to help in the effort.

• Resolve to express your "attitude of gratitude" to God and to others who are God's blessings to you through oral and written "thank yous."

Family Connection

• Plan a family "God's Wonders" outing. Visit a park, nature center, or other outdoor area to identify God's goodness and power in His world.

• Visit the library to check out books or videos on the natural or animal world. Read Psalm 148 together and then discuss how all creation praises and glorifies the Creator.

• Look at your family's history—pictures of grandparents, great-grandparents, and beyond. If known, share with your children stories of how your relatives provided for and cared for your generation. Thank God for the gift of family and for all others He has brought into our lives to love and care for us.

Closing Worship

Sing or read aloud the stanzas from "The Lord, My God, Be Praised" (*LW* 174).

> The Lord, my God, be praised,
> My light, my life from heaven;
> My maker, who to me
> Has soul and body given;
> My Father, who will shield
> And keep me day by day
> And make each moment yield
> New blessing on my way.

The Lord, my God, be praised,
My God, the everliving,
To whom the heav'nly host
Their laud and praise are giving.
The Lord, my God, be praised,
In whose great name I boast
God Father, God the Son,
And God the Holy Ghost.

For Next Week

Read the Second Article with Luther's explanation.

Session 6

Jesus—Lord

The Second Article

Law/Gospel Focus

The human condition is characterized by captivity—to sin, death, evil, and the devil. We cannot free ourselves; we have no resources, strength, or natural ability to bring about our salvation. The Son of God became flesh (John 1:14) and offered Himself as the sacrifice for the sins of the world. Jesus is Savior and Lord for all who believe God's Good News.

Opening Worship

Read responsively the following litany based on Psalm 47.

Leader: Clap your hands, all peoples! Shout to God with loud songs of joy!

Participants: **For the LORD, the Most High, is to be feared, a great King over all the earth.**

Leader: God has gone up with a shout, the LORD with the sound of a trumpet.

Participants: **Sing praises to God, sing praises! Sing praises to our King, sing praises!**

Leader: For God is the King of all the earth; sing praises with a psalm.

Participants: **God reigns over the nations; God sits on His holy throne.**

Free at Last

Frederick Douglass, the African-American abolitionist and orator, understood the tragedy and horror of slavery. For twenty-one years Douglass lived as a slave in Maryland. He knew the deplorable conditions his people faced daily as well as the mistreatment and hardship. Douglass also knew the yearnings of his fellow slaves. Every song they sang, he wrote in his autobiography, "was a testimony against slavery, and a prayer to God for deliverance from chains."

In his catechisms, Luther celebrates the Good News of God's salvation—freedom in Christ.

87. What hardships and horrors does slavery inflict on human beings?

88. What slaveries hold people in bondage today?

89. How do people seek "deliverance" from their chains in life?

That I May Be His Own

The Small Catechism

The Second Article

[I believe] in Jesus Christ, His only Son, our Lord, who was conceived by the Holy Spirit, born of the virgin Mary, suffered under Pontius Pilate, was crucified, died and was buried. He descended into hell. The third day He rose again from the dead. He ascended into heaven and sits at the right hand of God the Father Almighty. From thence He will come to judge the living and the dead.

What does this mean? I believe that Jesus Christ, true God, begotten of the Father from eternity, and also true man, born of the Virgin Mary, is my Lord. He has redeemed me, a lost and condemned creature, purchased and won me from all sins, from death, and from the power of the devil. He did this not with gold or silver, but with His holy, precious blood and with His innocent suffering and death, so that I may be His own, live under Him in His kingdom, and serve Him in everlasting righteousness, innocence, and blessedness, just as He is risen from the dead, lives and reigns to all eternity.

This is most certainly true.

The Large Catechism

Now, if you are asked, "What do you believe in the Second Article about Jesus Christ?" answer briefly,

"I believe that Jesus Christ, God's true Son, has become my Lord."

"But what does it mean to become Lord?"

"It is this. He has redeemed me from sin, from the devil, from death, and from all evil. For before I did not have a Lord or King, but was captive under the devil's power, condemned to death, stuck in sin and blindness" (see Ephesians 2:1–3).

For when we had been created by God the Father and had received from Him all kinds of good, the devil came and led us into disobedience, sin, death, and all evil (Genesis 3). So we fell under God's wrath and displeasure and were doomed to eternal damnation, just as we had merited and deserved. There was no counsel, help, or comfort until this only and eternal Son of God—in His immeasurable goodness—had compassion upon our misery and wretchedness. He came from heaven to help us (John 1:9). So those tyrants and jailers are all expelled now. In their place has come Jesus Christ, Lord of life, righteousness, every blessing, and salvation. He has delivered us poor, lost people from hell's jaws, has won us, has made us free (Romans 8:1–2), and has brought us again into the Father's favor and grace. He has taken us as His own property under His shelter and protection (Psalm 61:3–4) so that He may govern us by His righteousness, wisdom, power, life, and blessedness. (LC II 27–30)

Discussing the Texts

90. What titles of Jesus does Luther emphasize in his explanation to the Second Article?

91. What imagery does Luther use to describe the human condition? Tell why this imagery is relevant to every time and culture.

92. What imagery does Luther use to describe the work of Christ?

93. Describe the battle between Christ and His enemies.

94. Why is it important to highlight both the divine and human natures in Christ?

95. What statements in the Second Article show Christ in the state of humiliation? the state of exaltation?

96. How does Luther describe the cost of salvation?

97. For what purpose, according to Luther, has Christ redeemed us?

98. Describe how the Second Article and Luther's explanation proclaim the whole Good News of Jesus.

Our Redeemer

In God's plan of salvation, the slave becomes the liberator. Jesus, the Lord of the universe, takes on Himself the "form of a servant" and becomes obedient to death for our sake (Philippians 2:7). The Son of God, rich in authority, status, wisdom, and power, humbles Himself to die the death of a criminal. In Christ, God's people are set free and transferred from one kingdom—darkness and death—to another kingdom—light and life.

The Large Catechism

Let this, then, be the sum of this article: the little word *Lord* means simply the same as *redeemer*. It means the One who has brought us from Satan to God, from death to life, from sin to righteousness, and who preserves us in the same. But all the points that follow in this article serve no other purpose than to explain and express this redemption. They explain how and by whom it was accomplished. They explain how much it cost Him and what He spent and risked so that He might win us and bring us under His dominion. It explains that He became man (John 1:14), was conceived and born without sin (Hebrews 4:15), from the Holy Spirit and from the Virgin Mary (Luke 1:35), so that He might overcome sin. Further, it explains that He suffered, died, and was buried so that He might make satisfaction for me and pay what I owe (1 Corinthians 15:3–4), not with silver or gold, but with His own precious blood (1 Peter 1:18–19). And He did all this in order to become my Lord. He did none of these things for Himself, nor did He have any need for redemption. After that He rose again from the dead, swallowed up and devoured death (1 Corinthians 15:54), and finally ascended into heaven and assumed the government at the Father's right hand (1 Peter 3:22). He did these things so that the devil and all powers must be subject to Him and lie at His feet (Hebrews 10:12–13) until finally, at the Last Day, He will completely divide and separate us from the wicked world, the devil, death, sin, and such (Matthew 25:31–46; 13:24–30, 47–50).

Yes, the entire Gospel that we preach is based on this point, that we properly understand this article as that upon which our salvation and all our happiness rests. It is so rich and complete that we can never learn it fully. (LC II 31, 33)

99. Describe, in your own words, the "cost" of our salvation.

100. "All this in order to become my Lord." In what ways does the Gospel affect

your relationships with others?

your attitudes and performance at work?

your financial decisions?

your leisure activities?

101. What does Christ's resurrection, ascension, and exaltation mean for the Church's message and mission? for your personal ministry?

102. In what way is the Second Article *the* doctrine of the Christian faith?

103. What do you think Luther means when he says of the Second Article, "It is so rich and complete that we can never learn it fully"?

Both God and Man

Personal Reflection

- Read—without interruption—one of the four Gospels (Matthew, Mark, Luke, or John). Make a list of the passages that most powerfully speak to you about the deity and humanity of Christ.

- Purchase a book by C. S. Lewis or another classic Christian author. Highlight the truths about Jesus, His person, ministry, death and resurrection, and His ongoing ministry in the Church through His Word and Sacraments.

- Each day during the coming week reflect upon what it means for your life that Jesus is your Lord. Write your daily thoughts. At the end of the week review your writings.

Family Connection

- Make crosses from various materials around your house (wood, leather, plastic, rope, branches, etc.). If possible, use different colors and textures in the crosses. Display each family member's work around the house.

- Make bracelets with the letter beads JSL to stand for "Jesus, Savior and Lord." Purchase materials at a craft store, toy store, or novelty jewelry store.

- Set up or construct a nativity scene. Discuss as a family what it means to you that God's Son came to earth as a human baby, born in a manger.

Closing Worship

Sing or read aloud the stanzas from "All Hail the Power of Jesus' Name" (*LW* 272).

All hail the pow'r of Jesus' name!
Let angels prostrate fall;
Bring forth the royal diadem
And crown Him Lord of all. (*Repeat.*)

Crown Him, you martyrs of our God,
Who from His altar call;
Extol the stem of Jesse's rod
And crown Him Lord of all. (*Repeat.*)

For Next Week

Read the Third Article with Luther's explanation.

Session 7

The Holy Spirit—Sanctifier

The Third Article: The Holy Spirit

Law/Gospel Focus

By nature, all people are spiritually dead. We reject God's Word and are unable to receive His gift of salvation in Christ. But the Holy Spirit works through the Gospel and Sacraments to bring us to, and keep us in, faith. As Sanctifier, the Spirit creates saving faith in our hearts and establishes us in the new life.

Opening Worship

Read responsively the following litany based on Psalm 62.

Leader: For God alone my soul waits in silence; from Him comes my salvation.

Participants: **He only is my rock and my salvation, my fortress; I shall not be greatly shaken.**

Leader: For God alone, O my soul, wait in silence, for my hope is from Him.

Participants: **He only is my rock and my salvation, my fortress; I shall not be shaken.**

Leader: On God rests my salvation and my glory; my mighty rock, my refuge is God.

Participants: **Trust in Him at all times, O people; pour out your heart before Him, God is a refuge for us.**

I Can?

In the first century BC, the Roman poet Virgil wrote, "They are able who think they are able."

At the beginning of 1998, a new company slogan was released: "I can."

Human beings have always relied on their ability, ingenuity, and resources to meet the challenges of life and to open doors to success. For some people, nothing is beyond our scope and power.

In his catechisms, Luther points to God's grace and gift as our only hope for salvation.

104. In what sense is a positive attitude an important—essential—part of life?

105. In your experiences, what are the limitations to "I can"?

106. In what ways might "I can" lead to frustration and despair?

He Has Called Me

The Small Catechism

The Third Article

I believe in the Holy Spirit, the holy Christian Church, the communion of saints, the forgiveness of sins, the resurrection of the body, and the life everlasting. Amen.

What does this mean? I believe that I cannot by my own reason or strength believe in Jesus Christ, my Lord, or come to Him. But the Holy Spirit has called me by the Gospel, enlightened me with His gifts, sanctified and kept me in the true faith.

In the same way He calls, gathers, enlightens, and sanctifies the whole Christian Church on earth and keeps it with Jesus Christ in the one true faith.

In this Christian Church He daily and richly forgives all my sins and the sins of all believers.

On the Last Day He will raise up me and all the dead and will give eternal life to me and to all believers in Christ.

This is most certainly true.

The Large Catechism

But God's Spirit alone is called the Holy Spirit, that is, He who has sanctified and still sanctifies us. For just as the Father is called "Creator" and the Son is called "Redeemer," so the Holy Spirit, from His work, must be called "Sanctifier," or "One who makes holy."

"But how is such sanctifying done?"

Answer, "The Son receives dominion, by which He wins us, through His birth, death, resurrection, and so on. In a similar way, the Holy Spirit causes our sanctification by the following: the communion of saints or the Christian Church, the forgiveness of sins, the resurrection of the body, and the life everlasting. That means He leads us first into His holy congregation and places us in the bosom of the Church. Through the Church He preaches to us and brings us to Christ."

Neither you nor I could ever know anything about Christ, or believe on Him, and have Him for our Lord, unless it were offered to us and granted to our hearts by the Holy Spirit through the preaching of the Gospel (1 Corinthians 12:3; Galatians 4:6). The work of redemption is done and accomplished (John 19:30). Christ has acquired and gained the treasure for us by His suffering, death, resurrection, and so on (Colossians 2:3). But if the work remained concealed so that no one knew about it, then it would be useless and lost. So that this treasure might not stay buried, but be received and enjoyed, God has caused the Word to go forth and be proclaimed. In the Word He has the Holy Spirit bring this treasure home and make it our own. Therefore, sanctifying is just bringing us to Christ so we receive this good, which we could not get ourselves (1 Peter 3:18). (LC II 36–39)

Discussing the Texts

107. How does Luther describe the person and work of the Holy Spirit?

108. What does *sanctify* mean? How does Luther apply the word *sanctify* to the work of the Holy Spirit?

109. Reason and strength are gifts from God. In what ways are they blessings in life? In what ways are they useless in spiritual matters?

110. Explain the following descriptions of the Spirit's work: called me by the Gospel

enlightened me with His gifts

sanctified and kept me in the true faith

111. In what sense, according to Luther, is the work of Christ *finished*? How does Christ's work *continue today*?

112. How do you know that the Holy Spirit has been at work in your life? How do you know His work is continuing in your life, even now?

113. Describe how a child of God by faith in Christ Jesus lives the sanctified life in response to the First Article? the Second Article?

114. How does God "[send] forth and proclaim" His Word today? How is the Holy Spirit at work in these ways?

God's Secret Wisdom

Human reason and strength are worthless in spiritual matters. On our own, we cannot understand God's truth, and we have no power to believe His promises. "No eye has seen, nor ear heard, nor the heart of man imagined, what God has prepared for those who love Him," St. Paul writes, "these things God has revealed to us through the Spirit" (1 Corinthians 2:9–10).

The love of God revealed in Jesus Christ is the mystery of the ages—God's secret wisdom. In the gift of the Holy Spirit, by water and the Word, God claims us as His children and creates saving faith in our hearts. The Spirit works in and through the Gospel to keep us "in Christ."

The Large Catechism

In short, the whole Gospel and all the offices of Christianity belong here, which also must be preached and taught without ceasing. God's grace is secured through Christ (John 1:17), and sanctification is wrought by the Holy Spirit through God's Word in the unity of the Christian Church. Yet because of our flesh, which we bear about with us, we are never without sin (Romans 7:23–24).

Everything, therefore, in the Christian Church is ordered toward this goal: we shall daily receive in the Church nothing but the forgiveness of sin through the Word and signs, to comfort and encourage our consciences as long as we live here. So even though we have sins, the grace of the Holy Spirit does not allow them to harm us. For we are in the Christian Church, where there is nothing but continuous, uninterrupted forgiveness of sin. This is because God forgives us and because we forgive, bear with, and help one another (Galatians 6:1–2).

. . . For now we are only half pure and holy. So the Holy Spirit always has some reason to continue His work in us through the Word. He must daily administer forgiveness until we reach the life to come. At that time there will be no more forgiveness, but only perfectly pure and holy people (1 Corinthians 13:10). We will be full of godliness and righteousness, removed and free from sin, death, and all evil, in a new, immortal, and glorified body (1 Corinthians 15:43, 53).

You see, all this is the Holy Spirit's office and work. He begins and daily increases holiness upon earth through these two things: the Christian Church and the forgiveness of sin. But in our death He will accomplish it altogether in an instant (1 Corinthians 15:52) and will forever preserve us therein by the last two parts [of the Creed]. (LC II 54–55, 58–59)

115. "The whole Gospel . . . must be preached and taught without ceasing." What does it mean in your life that you still "bear" your sinful nature?

116. The Holy Spirit, Luther comments, makes certain that sin does not "harm us." Describe how this is true on earth and for eternity.

117. Salvation is God's gift from start to finish! How would you respond to these statements?

"It's my responsibility to accept the Gospel."

"It's my responsibility to live as a Christian."

"It's my responsibility to keep my faith to the end of my life."

118. Describe how Word and Sacraments "comfort and encourage" our conscience when used on a regular basis.

Supporting the Faith

Personal Reflection

- Write a note of appreciation to your godparents or Christian sponsors who have supported you in the faith. Share your gratitude for their encouragement and prayers. Sign the note with your confirmation verse or other Scripture passage.

- Reflect on the gifts God has given to you. Ask, "How can I serve Christ and my congregation in the years ahead?" Meditate on Romans 12:1–8 and 1 Corinthians 12. Talk to your pastor about opportunities to serve God's people.

- Look for ways to "[send] forth and proclaim" God's Word at work, in your neighborhood, or through your community.

Family Connection

- Walk through your home, your neighborhood, or a shopping center identifying all the sources and "users" of power. Talk together about the power the Spirit brings to each Christian.

- On large poster board, trace the shape of a dove. Invite each family member to write a blessing from God the Holy Spirit in his or her life. Or write brief prayers to the Holy Spirit, asking for the blessings of faith, hope, and love.

- Identify Christians who evidence one or more of the "fruit of the Spirit." Thank God for their witness to Christ and His Good News.

Closing Worship

Sing or read aloud the stanza from "O Holy Spirit, Enter In" (*LW* 160).

O Holy Spirit, enter in,
And in our hearts Your work begin,
And make our hearts Your dwelling.
Sun of the soul, O Light divine,
Around and in us brightly shine,
Your strength in us upwelling.
In Your radiance Life from heaven
Now is given Overflowing,
Gift of gifts beyond all knowing.

O mighty Rock, O Source of life,
Let Your good Word in doubt and strife
Be in us strongly burning
That we be faithful unto death
And live in love and holy faith,
From You true wisdom learning.
Lord, Your mercy On us shower;

By Your power Christ confessing,
We will cherish all Your blessing.

For Next Week

Read the Third Article with Luther's explanation.

Session 8

A Community in Christ

The Third Article: The Holy Christian Church

Law/Gospel Focus

Sin destroys relationships. By disobeying God's Word, Adam and Eve separated themselves from perfect fellowship with God and from one another. Although we live in a world of brokenness and alienation, the Gospel brings us into a new relationship with God through faith. In the Church God gives His gifts of forgiveness and eternal life to everyone who trusts in Jesus.

Opening Worship

Read responsively the following litany based on Psalm 84.

Leader: How lovely is Your dwelling place, O LORD of hosts!

Participants: **My soul longs, yes, faints, for the courts of the LORD; my heart and my flesh sing for joy to the living God.**

Leader: Blessed are those who dwell in Your house, ever singing Your praise.

Participants: **Blessed are those whose strength is in You.**

Leader: For a day in Your courts is better than a thousand elsewhere.

Participants: **O LORD of hosts, blessed is the one who trusts in You!**

Individuals in Community

"We have learned that we cannot live alone, at peace," Franklin D. Roosevelt remarked during his fourth inaugural address in January 1945. "We have learned to be citizens of the world, members of the human community."

For nations and people alike, isolation is often a fearful course. In many ways, we are connected to each another and dependent on one another—individuals in community.

In his catechisms, Luther explains God's purpose in calling His people together in the Church.

119. Describe the types of "communities" of which you are a member.

120. In what ways is community a blessing to human life?

121. What problems and concerns may arise when persons and families live in isolation?

Christian Community

The Small Catechism

The Third Article

I believe in the Holy Spirit, the holy Christian Church, the communion of saints, the forgiveness of sins, the resurrection of the body, and the life everlasting. Amen.

What does this mean? I believe that I cannot by my own reason or strength believe in Jesus Christ, my Lord, or come to Him. But the Holy Spirit has called me by the Gospel, enlightened me with His gifts, sanctified and kept me in the true faith.

In the same way He calls, gathers, enlightens, and sanctifies the whole Christian Church on earth and keeps it with Jesus Christ in the one true faith.

In this Christian Church He daily and richly forgives all my sins and the sins of all believers.

On the Last Day He will raise up me and all the dead and will give eternal life to me and to all believers in Christ.

This is most certainly true.

The Large Catechism

You may be asked, "What do you mean by the words *I believe in the Holy Spirit*?"

You can then answer, "I believe that the Holy Spirit makes me holy, as His name implies."

"But how does He accomplish this, or what are His method and means to this end?"

Answer, "By the Christian Church, the forgiveness of sins, the resurrection of the body, and the life everlasting. For in the first place, the Spirit has His own congregation in the world, which is the mother that conceives and bears every Christian through God's Word (Galatians 4:26). Through the Word He reveals and preaches, He illumines and enkindles hearts, so that they understand, accept, cling to, and persevere in the Word" (1 Corinthians 2:12). (LC II 40–42)

But this is the meaning and substance of this addition: I believe that there is upon earth a little holy group and congregation of pure saints, under one head, even Christ (Ephesians 1:22). This group is called together by the Holy Spirit in one faith, one mind, and understanding, with many different gifts, yet agreeing in love, without sects or schisms (Ephesians 4:5–8, 11). I am also a part and member of this same group, a sharer and joint owner of all the goods it possesses (Romans 8:17). I am brought to it and incorporated into it by the Holy Spirit through having heard and continuing to hear God's Word (Galatians 3:1–2), which is the beginning of entering it. In the past, before we had attained to this, we were altogether of the devil, knowing nothing about God and about Christ (Romans 3:10–12). So, until the Last Day, the Holy Spirit abides with the holy congregation or Christendom (John 14:17). Through this congregation He brings us to Christ and He teaches and preaches to us the Word (John 14:26). By the Word He works and promotes sanctification, causing this congregation daily to grow and to become strong in the faith and its fruit, which He produces (Galatians 5).

We further believe that in this Christian Church we have forgiveness of sin, which is wrought through the holy Sacraments and

Absolution (Matthew 26:28; Mark 1:4; John 20:23) and through all kinds of comforting promises from the entire Gospel. Therefore, whatever ought to be preached about the Sacraments belongs here. In short, the whole Gospel and all the offices of Christianity belong here, which also must be preached and taught without ceasing. (LC II 51–54)

Discussing the Texts

122. In what ways is the Church the Spirit's "own congregation in the world"?

123. What different meanings do we often apply to the word "church"? How do the meanings complement each other?

124. What, according to the Small Catechism, does the Holy Spirit do in and for the Church?

125. What truths does Luther note about the Church in the Large Catechism?

126. Describe how the Church is one. Describe the diversity also existing within.

127. In what ways does God "daily and richly" forgive sin "in this Christian Church"?

128. In what ways do you regularly receive the Word through which the Holy Spirit works?

129. What does the Holy Spirit do at the Last Day? How is this gift the full and final blessing of Christ's work?

130. What does Luther mean by saying that "in this Christian Church we have forgiveness of sin"?

Life Together

Edward Everett paints a picture of life in community.

We ask the leaf, "Are you complete in yourself?" and the leaf answers, "No, my life is in the branches." We ask the branch, and the branch answers, "No, my life is in the trunk." We ask the trunk, and it answers, "No, my life is in the root." We ask the root, and it answers, "No, my life is in the trunk and the branches and the leaves." So it is. . . . Nothing is completely and merely individual.

In His death and resurrection, Christ has created and called together a new community: His Church. Baptized into His saving work, we live in fellowship with God and with one another. We live in forgiveness, joy, and the hope of salvation *together*—members of one body, branches of the one vine, sheep of the one flock.

The Large Catechism

For we have already received creation. Redemption, too, is finished. But the Holy Spirit carries on His work without ceasing to the Last Day. For that purpose He has appointed a congregation upon earth by which He speaks and does everything. For He has not yet brought together all His Christian Church (John 10:16) or granted all forgiveness. Therefore, we believe in Him who daily brings us into the fellowship of this Christian Church through the Word. Through the same Word and the forgiveness of sins He bestows, increases, and strengthens faith. So when He has done it all, and we abide in this and die to the world and to all evil, He may finally make us perfectly and forever holy. Even now we expect this in faith through the Word.

See, here you have the entire divine essence, will, and work shown most completely in quite short and yet rich words. In these words all our wisdom stands, which surpasses and exceeds the wisdom, mind, and reason of all people (1 Corinthians 1:18–25). The whole world with all diligence has struggled to figure out what God is, what He has in mind and does. Yet the world has never been able to grasp the knowledge and understanding of any of these things. But here we have everything in richest measure. For here in all three articles God has revealed Himself and opened the deepest abyss of His fatherly heart and His pure, inexpressible love (Ephesians 3:18–19). He has created us for this very reason, that He might redeem and sanctify us. In addition to giving and imparting to us everything in heaven and upon earth, He has even given to us His Son and the Holy Spirit, who brings us to Himself (Romans 8:14, 32). For (as explained above) we could never grasp the knowledge of the Father's grace and favor except through the Lord Christ. Jesus is a mirror of the fatherly heart (John 14:9; Colossians 1:15; Hebrews 1:3), outside of whom we see nothing but an angry and terrible Judge. But we couldn't know anything about Christ either, unless it had been revealed by the Holy Spirit (1 Corinthians 2:12). (LC II 61–65)

131. The Spirit, Luther writes, is *always* working. How is this truth a comfort in your faith? an encouragement in the Church's ministry?

132. In what ways have the Church and your congregation been a blessing in your life?

133. "He has not yet brought together all His Christian Church." Explain.

134. Describe how the Apostles' Creed reveals, as Luther notes, "the divine essence, will, and work."

135. The world has "never been able to grasp" who God is, what God thinks, or what God does. Give examples.

136. Although the Holy Spirit brought you to faith in Christ, the Spirit uses people to bring us the Gospel throughout our lives. Who has shared with you—and modeled for you—Christ's love? How can you bring the Gospel to others?

Family of Faith

Personal Reflection

- Read or investigate the history of your congregation, focusing on how God worked to establish your faith family.

- After worship, explore the building design and art in your church's sanctuary. Reflect on the structure, design, and symbols and the message they project to members and nonmembers alike.

- *Give* is central to *forgive*. God gives His love and mercy in Christ that we may forgive and share His gifts with others. Meditate on forgiveness and its place in your life.

Family Connection

• After worship, take a few minutes to walk around your congregation's facility. Note the names and purposes of the various rooms. Plan a time when you can return to help "spruce up" a part of your church.

• Talk about the activities your family does to celebrate your relationship as members of the fellowship of believers. Possibilities include studying God's Word, praying, forgiving one another, and attending worship together.

• As a family join hands and invite each person to pray, asking God's special blessings for the person on his or her left.

Closing Worship

Sing or read aloud the stanzas from "The Church's One Foundation" (*LW* 289).

> The Church's one foundation
> Is Jesus Christ, her Lord;
> She is His new creation
> By water and the Word.
> From heav'n He came and sought her
> To be His holy bride;
> With His own blood He bought her,
> And for her life He died.
>
> Elect from ev'ry nation,
> Yet one o'er all the earth;
> Her charter of salvation:
> One Lord, one faith, one birth.
> One holy name she blesses,
> Partakes one holy food,
> And to one hope she presses
> With ev'ry grace endued.

For Next Week

Read the Introduction through Third Petition of the Lord's Prayer with Luther's explanations.

Session 9

The Father's Heart: God's Name, Kingdom, and Will

The Lord's Prayer: The Introduction—Third Petition

Law/Gospel Focus

Prayer is heart-to-heart conversation with the living God. God invites and commands us to pray. Because of sin, though, we neglect to call on God in our need; because of sin, we pray with selfish motives and ambitions. In His love, God forgives us through Christ. Our gracious Father gives us His Spirit and the Word that we may pray regularly and boldly in Jesus' name.

Opening Worship

Read responsively the following litany based on Psalm 20.

Leader: May the Lord answer you in the day of trouble!

Participants: **May the name of the God of Jacob protect you!**

Leader: May He send you help from the sanctuary and give you support from Zion!

Participants: **May He remember all your offerings and regard with favor your burnt sacrifices.**

Leader: May He grant you your heart's desire and fulfill all your plans.

Participants: **May the Lord fulfill all your petitions.**

Leader: Some trust in chariots and some in horses,

Participants: **But we trust in the name of the LORD our God.**

Blessings and Promises

In poll after poll, over 90 percent of Americans report that they "pray regularly."

Physicians recommend prayer for their patients. Newspapers and magazines report stories of changed lives and miraculous events. Studies indicate that medical patients do better when others are praying for them even when the patients do not know it.

In his catechisms, Luther focuses on the blessings and promises God gives as His children pray the Lord's Prayer.

137. Why do people pray? Why do they *not* pray?

138. When do people generally pray? What do they generally pray for?

139. In what ways is it difficult to pray alone? in public?

Asking with Confidence

The Small Catechism

The Introduction

Our Father who art in heaven.

What does this mean? By these words God would tenderly encourage us to believe that He is our true Father and that we are His true children, so that we may ask Him confidently with all assurance, as dear children ask their dear father.

The First Petition

Hallowed be Thy name.

What does this mean? God's name is indeed holy in itself. But we pray in this petition that it may become holy among us also.

How is this done? When the Word of God is taught in its truth and purity and we as the children of God also lead holy lives in accordance with it. To this end help us, dear Father in heaven. But anyone who teaches and lives other than by what God's Word teaches profanes the name of God among us. From this preserve us, heavenly Father.

The Second Petition

Thy kingdom come.

What does this mean? The kingdom of God comes indeed without our prayer, of itself. But we pray in this petition that it may come to us also.

How is this done? When our heavenly Father gives us His Holy Spirit, so that by His grace we believe His holy Word and lead a godly life here in time and there in eternity.

The Third Petition

Thy will be done on earth as it is in heaven.

What does this mean? The good and gracious will of God is done indeed without our prayer. But we pray in this petition that it may be done among us also.

How is this done? When God breaks and hinders every evil counsel and will that would not let us hallow the name of God nor let His kingdom come, such as the will of the devil, the world, and our flesh. Instead, He strengthens and keeps us steadfast in His Word and in faith until we die. This is His gracious and good will.

The Large Catechism

The first thing to know is that it is our duty to pray because of God's commandment. For that's what we heard in the Second Commandment, "You shall not take the name of the LORD your God in vain" (Exodus 20:7). We are required to praise that holy name and call upon it in every need, or to pray. To call upon God's name is nothing other than to pray (e.g., 1 Kings 18:24). Prayer is just as strictly and seriously commanded as all other commandments: to have no other God, not to kill, not to steal, and so on. (LC III 5–6)

The First Petition

"But what does it mean to pray that His name may be holy? Is it not holy already?"

Answer, "Yes, it is always holy in its nature, but in our use it is not holy." For God's name was given to us when we became Christians and were baptized (Matthew 28:19). So we are called God's children and have the Sacraments, by which He connects us with Himself so that everything that belongs to God must serve for our use (Romans 8:16–17).

Now, here is a great need that we ought to be most concerned about. This name should have its proper honor; it should be valued holy and grand as the greatest treasure and sanctuary that we have. As godly children we should pray that God's name, which is already holy in heaven, may also be and remain holy with us upon earth and in all the world.

"But how does it become holy among us?"

Answer, as plainly as it can be said: "When both our doctrine and life are godly and Christian." Since we call God our Father in this prayer, it is our duty always to act and behave ourselves as godly children, that He may not receive shame, but honor and praise from us. (LC III 37–39)

The Second Petition

"But what is God's kingdom?"

Answer, "Nothing other than what we learned in the Creed: God sent His Son, Jesus Christ, our Lord, into the world to redeem and deliver us from the devil's power (1 John 3:8). He sent Him to bring us to Himself and to govern us as a King of righteousness, life, and salvation against sin, death, and an evil conscience. For this reason He has also given His Holy Spirit, who is to bring these things home to us by His holy Word and to illumine and strengthen us in the faith by His power."

We pray here in the first place that this may happen with us. We pray that His name may be so praised through God's holy Word and a Christian life that we who have accepted it may abide and daily grow in it, and that it may gain approval and acceptance among other people. We pray that it may go forth with power throughout the world (2 Thessalonians 3:1). We pray that many may find entrance into the kingdom of grace (John 3:5), be made partakers of redemption (Colossians 1:12–14), and be led to it by the Holy Spirit (Romans 8:14), so that we may all together remain forever in the one kingdom now begun. (LC III 51–52)

The Third Petition

In a good government it is not only necessary that there be those who build and govern well. It is also necessary to have those who defend, offer protection, and maintain it firmly. So in God's kingdom, although we have prayed for the greatest need—for the Gospel, faith, and the Holy Spirit, that He may govern us and redeem us from the devil's power—we must also pray that God's will be done. For there will be strange events if we are to abide in God's will. We shall have to suffer many thrusts and blows on that account from everything that seeks to oppose and prevent the fulfillment of the first two petitions. . . .

So there is just as great a need, as in all the other petitions, that we pray without ceasing, "Dear Father, Your will be done, not the devil's will or our enemies' or anything that would persecute and suppress Your holy Word or hinder Your kingdom. Grant that we may bear with patience and overcome whatever is to be endured because of Your Word and kingdom, so that our poor flesh may not yield or fall away because of weakness or sluggishness." (LC III 61–67)

Discussing the Texts

140. What does the Lord's Prayer reveal about God's relationship to us and our relationship to Him?

141. Explain the appropriateness of praying "confidently with all assurance."

142. How is the First Petition connected to the Second Commandment?

143. In what ways do we dishonor God's name?

144. In what sense is God's name holy among His people?

145. What, according to Luther, is God's kingdom? How does it come to us?

146. How is God's kingdom a present reality? How is God's kingdom a future promise?

147. List the words and phrases that describe God's will.

148. How does Luther relate the Third Petition to our struggles with sin, the devil, and the world?

Powerful Petitions

An Early Church pastor and teacher wrote, "What deep mysteries are contained in the Lord's Prayer. How many and great they are! They are expressed in a few words, but they are rich in spiritual power so that nothing is left out; every petition and prayer we have to make is included. It is a compendium of heavenly doctrine" (St. Cyprian).

The Lord who gave these petitions is the Savior who makes our prayers possible. In His death, Jesus forgives us and frees us to call to our heavenly Father in every need. In His resurrection, Jesus raises us to life and salvation that we might praise our gracious God for all His blessings.

The Large Catechism

> Every one of us should form the daily habit from his youth of praying for all his needs. He should pray whenever he notices anything affecting his interests or that of other people among whom he may live. He should pray for preachers, the government, neighbors, household servants, and always (as we have said) to hold up to God His commandment and promise, knowing that He will not have them disregarded. . . .
>
> Let this be said as encouragement, so that people may learn, first of all, to value prayer as something great and precious and to make a proper distinction between babbling and praying for something. (LC III 28–33)

The First Petition

> So you see that in this petition we pray for exactly what God demands in the Second Commandment. We pray that His name not be taken in vain to swear, curse, lie, deceive, and so on, but be used well for God's praise and honor. For whoever uses God's name for any sort of wrong profanes and desecrates this holy name. This is how it used to be when a Church was considered desecrated, when a murder or any other crime had been committed in it. . . . as though they were holy in themselves—when they became unholy by misuse. So this point is easy and clear if only the language is understood: to hallow means the same as to praise, magnify, and honor both in word and deed.
>
> Here, now, learn what great need there is for such prayer. Because we see how full the world is of sects and false teachers, who all wear the holy name as a cover and sham for their doctrines of devils (1 Timothy 4:1), we should by all means pray without ceasing (1 Thessalonians 5:17) and cry out and call upon God against all people who preach and believe falsely. We should pray against whatever opposes and persecutes our Gospel and pure doctrine and would suppress it. (LC III 45–47)

The Second Petition

> For the coming of God's kingdom to us happens in two ways: (a) here in time through the Word and faith (Matthew 13); and (b) in

eternity forever through revelation (Luke 19:11; 1 Peter 1:4–5). Now we pray for both these things. We pray that the kingdom may come to those who are not yet in it, and, by daily growth that it may come to us who have received it, both now and hereafter in eternal life. All this is nothing other than saying, "Dear Father, we pray, give us first Your Word, so that the Gospel may be preached properly throughout the world. Second, may the Gospel be received in faith and work and live in us, so that through the Word and the Holy Spirit's power (Romans 15:18–19), Your kingdom may triumph among us. And we pray that the devil's kingdom be put down (Luke 11:17–20), so that he may have no right or power over us (Luke 10:17–19; Colossians 1), until at last his power may be utterly destroyed. So sin, death, and hell shall be exterminated (Revelation 20:13–14). Then we may live forever in perfect righteousness and blessedness" (Ephesians 4:12–13).

From this you see that we do not pray here for a crust of bread or a temporal, perishable good. Instead, we pray for an eternal inestimable treasure and everything that God Himself possesses. (LC III 53–55)

The Third Petition

Look, we have in these three petitions, in the simplest way, the needs that relate to God Himself. Yet they are all for our sakes. Whatever we pray concerns us alone. As we have said before, we pray that what must be done without us anyway may also be done in us. As His name must be hallowed and His kingdom come whether we pray or not, so also His will must be done and succeed. This is true even though the devil with all his followers raise a great riot, are angry and rage against it, and try to exterminate the Gospel completely. But for our own sakes we must pray that, even against their fury, His will be done without hindrance among us also. We pray so that they may not be able to accomplish anything and that we may remain firm against all violence and persecution and submit to God's will. (LC III 68)

149. In Christ, we call God "our Father." List the comforts and blessings we receive from this relationship.

150. To "praise, magnify, and honor" God in word and deed is our calling in Christ. How does this express our life's priorities?

151. In what ways is it difficult to pray, "Thy will be done"?

152. What thoughts come to mind when you pray for God's kingdom to come here on earth? hereafter in eternity?

153. What evidence can you give that God is working His will in your life?

Into Your Hands

Personal Reflection

- Write out Luther's Morning Prayer on a note card. Tape the note card on your bathroom mirror and pray the prayer aloud every morning.

   I thank You, my heavenly Father, through Jesus Christ, Your dear Son, that You have kept me this night from all harm and danger; and I pray that You would keep me this day also from sin and every evil, that all my doings and life may please You. For into Your hands I commend myself, my body and soul, and all things. Let Your holy angel be with me, that the evil foe may have no power over me. Amen.

- Purchase a book on prayer or a book of prayers. If possible, use the ideas or prayers during your personal devotion time.

- Think and pray about God's will for your life. Plan to reference

God's will in your conversations saying, "God willing" or "If the Lord wills" (James 4:15).

Family Connection

- Start a weeklong "prayer chain" with strips of colored paper. Each family member writes a prayer request on one strip. Loop and fasten (staple or glue) the strips of paper together to make a chain. Be sure to pray the different requests!

- Buy knot or twist pretzels for snacks. Comment that pretzels originated as reminders to pray. When family members want a snack, encourage them to offer a silent prayer for other family members and friends.

- Talk about how God's will has been done among the members of your family.

Closing Worship

Sing or read aloud these stanzas from "What a Friend We Have in Jesus" (*LW* 516).

> What a friend we have in Jesus,
> All our sins and griefs to bear!
> What a privilege to carry
> Ev'rything to God in prayer!
> Oh, what peace we often forfeit;
> Oh, what needless pain we bear—
> All because we do not carry
> Ev'rything to God in prayer!
>
> Have we trials and temptations?
> Is there trouble anywhere?
> We should never be discouraged—
> Take it to the Lord in prayer.
> Can we find a friend so faithful
> Who will all our sorrows share?
> Jesus knows our ev'ry weakness—
> Take it to the Lord in prayer.

For Next Week

Read the Fourth Petition through Conclusion of the Lord's Prayer with Luther's explanation.

Session 10

The Father's Gifts: Daily Bread, Forgiveness, and Protection

The Lord's Prayer: The Fourth Petition— Conclusion

Law/Gospel Focus

God is the giver of all good gifts. Yet because of sin, we ignore or despise His blessings and His offer to provide for His creation. In Christ, the heavenly Father shows His love and forgiveness. He encourages us to pray for our physical and spiritual needs, and He promises to hear and answer us.

Opening Worship

Read responsively the following litany based on Psalm 31.

Leader: In You, O LORD, do I take refuge;

Participants: **Let me never be put to shame; in Your righteousness deliver me.**

Leader: Incline Your ear to me; rescue me speedily!

Participants: **Be a rock of refuge for me, a strong fortress to save me!**

Leader: For You are my rock and my fortress; and for Your name's sake You lead and guide me.

Participants: **You take me out of the net they have hidden for me, for You are my refuge.**

Leader: Into Your hand I commit my spirit;

Participants: **You have redeemed me, O LORD, faithful God.**

What Do You Need?

A Christian poet has written, "In prayer one sees life as God sees it and relates his own little life and his own little needs to the needs and life of humanity" (Robert L. Kahn).

What are our needs? What are humanity's needs? Who will provide for the necessities of life?

In his explanation to the Lord's Prayer, Luther focuses on God's rich gifts in Christ for all our physical and spiritual needs.

154. In what ways do people look at "basic needs" differently?

155. How have needs changed over the past hundred years? thousand years?

156. How are your individual needs related to the needs and life of all people?

Good Gifts

The Small Catechism

The Fourth Petition

Give us this day our daily bread.

What does this mean? God gives daily bread, even without our prayer, to all wicked people; but we pray in this petition that He would lead us to realize this and to receive our daily bread with thanksgiving.

What is meant by daily bread? Everything that belongs to the support and needs of the body, such as food, drink, clothing, shoes, house, home, field, cattle, money, goods, a pious spouse, pious children, pious servants, pious and faithful rulers, good government, good weather, peace, health, discipline, honor, good friends, faithful neighbors, and the like.

The Fifth Petition

And forgive us our trespasses as we forgive those who trespass against us.

What does this mean? We pray in this petition that our Father in heaven would not look upon our sins nor deny such petitions on account of them. We are not worthy of any of the things for which we pray, neither have we deserved them. But we pray that He would grant them all to us by grace. For we daily sin much and indeed deserve nothing but punishment. So will we truly, on our part, also heartily forgive and readily do good to those who sin against us.

The Sixth Petition

And lead us not into temptation.

What does this mean? God indeed tempts no one. But we pray in this petition that God would guard and keep us, so that the devil, the world, and our flesh may not deceive us nor seduce us into false belief, despair, and other great shame and vice. Though we are attacked by these things, we pray that still we may finally overcome them and gain the victory.

The Seventh Petition

But deliver us from evil.

What does this mean? We pray in this petition, as in a summary, that our Father in heaven would deliver us from all kinds of evil, of body and soul, property and honor. And finally, when our last hour shall come, we pray that He would grant us a blessed end and graciously take us from this vale of tears to Himself into heaven.

The Conclusion

For Thine is the kingdom and the power and the glory forever and ever.* Amen.

What does this mean? I should be certain that these petitions are acceptable to our Father in heaven and are heard by Him. For He Himself has commanded us to pray this way and has promised that He will hear us. Amen, Amen; that is, "Yes, yes, it shall be so."

* *These words were not in Luther's Small Catechism.*

84

The Large Catechism

The Fourth Petition

To sum things up, this petition includes everything that belongs to our entire life in the world, for we need daily bread because of life alone. It is not only necessary for our life that our body have food and clothes and other necessaries. It is also necessary that we spend our days in peace and quiet among the people with whom we live and have dealings in daily business and conversation and all sorts of doings (1 Thessalonians 4:11; 2 Thessalonians 3:12; 1 Timothy 2:2). In short, this petition applies both to the household and also to the neighborly or civil relationship and government. Where these two things are hindered so that they do not prosper as they should, the necessaries of life also are hindered. Ultimately, life cannot be maintained. There is, indeed, the greatest need to pray for earthly authority and government. By them, most of all, God preserves for us our daily bread and all the comforts of this life. Though we have received from God all good things in abundance, we are not able to keep any of them or use them in security and happiness if He did not give us a permanent and peaceful government. For where there are dissension, strife, and war, there the daily bread is already taken away or is at least hindered. (LC III 73–74)

The Fifth Petition

It is, therefore, the intent of this petition that God would not regard our sins and hold up to us what we daily deserve. But we pray that He would deal graciously with us and forgive, as He has promised, and so grant us a joyful and confident conscience to stand before Him in prayer (Hebrews 10:22). For where the heart is not in a right relationship with God, or cannot take such confidence, it will not dare to pray anymore. Such a confident and joyful heart can spring from nothing else than the certain knowledge of the forgiveness of sin (Psalm 32:1–2; Romans 4:7–8). (LC III 92)

The Sixth Petition

Temptation . . . is of three kinds: of the flesh, of the world, and of the devil. For we dwell in the flesh and carry the old Adam about our neck. He exerts himself and encourages us daily to unchastity, laziness, gluttony and drunkenness, greed and deception, to defraud our neighbor and to overcharge him (Galatians 5:19–21; Colossians 3:5–8). In short, the old Adam encourages us to have all kinds of evil lusts, which cling to us by nature and to which we are moved by the society, the example, and what we hear and see of other people. They often wound and inflame even an innocent heart.

Next comes the world, which offends us in word and deed. It drives us to anger and impatience. In short, there is nothing but hatred and envy, hostility, violence and wrong, unfaithfulness, vengeance, cursing, railing, slander, pride and haughtiness, with useless finery, honor, fame, and power. No one is willing to be the least. Everyone desires to sit at the head of the group and to be seen before all (Luke 14:7–11).

Then comes the devil, pushing and provoking in all directions. But he especially agitates matters that concern the conscience and spiritual affairs. He leads us to despise and disregard both God's Word and works. He tears us away from faith, hope, and love (1 Corinthians 13:13), and he brings us into misbelief, false security, and stubbornness. Or, on the other hand, he leads us to despair, denial of God, blasphemy, and innumerable other shocking things. These are snares and nets (2 Timothy 2:26), indeed, real fiery darts that are shot like poison into the heart, not by flesh and blood, but by the devil (Ephesians 6:12, 16). (LC III 101–4)

The Seventh Petition

It looks like Jesus was speaking about the devil, like He would summarize every petition in one. So the entire substance of all our prayer is directed against our chief enemy. For it is he who hinders among us everything that we pray for: God's name or honor, God's kingdom and will, our daily bread, a cheerful good conscience, and so forth.

Therefore, we finally sum it all up and say, "Dear Father, grant that we be rid of all these disasters." But there is also included in this petition whatever evil may happen to us under the devil's kingdom: poverty, shame, death, and, in short, all the agonizing misery and heartache of which there is such an unnumbered multitude on the earth. (LC III 113–15).

Discussing the Texts

157. What specific blessings for this life do you most appreciate? What would you add to Luther's list?

158. In what ways is our "daily bread" connected to larger contexts—our community, the nation, and global concerns?

159. Is the "greatest need to pray for our earthly authority and government"? Explain your answer.

160. Why are Christians often reluctant to pray for government leaders?

161. Describe the connection between God's forgiving us and our forgiving others.

162. "We daily sin much." Why is it important to acknowledge and accept this truth?

163. In what ways is a "confident and joyful heart" dependent on the forgiveness of sins?

164. How does Luther describe the temptations Christians face?

165. In what ways does the Seventh Petition summarize the whole Lord's Prayer?

Father Knows Best

A simple Christian prayer asks God, "Behold my needs which I know not myself."

As the first three petitions centered on God, the last four petitions of the Lord's Prayer revolve around our human needs: our earthly concerns, our spiritual requirements, and the dangers and troubles we face throughout life. In all these areas, however, God provides. God has shown His mercy in Christ, and gives His blessings of forgiveness and salvation to sustain us through all circumstances. Through faith, we open our hands, and He satisfies us with every good gift.

The Large Catechism

The Fourth Petition

You see, in this way, God wishes to show us how He cares for us in all our need and faithfully provides also for our earthly support. He abundantly grants and preserves these things, even for the wicked and rogues (Matthew 5:45). Yet, He wishes that we pray for these goods in order that we may recognize that we receive them from His hand and may feel His fatherly goodness toward us in them (Psalm 104:28; 145:16). For when He withdraws His hand, nothing can prosper or be maintained in the end. Indeed, we daily see this and experience it. (LC III 82–83)

The Fifth Petition

[God] has promised that we shall be sure that everything is forgiven and pardoned, in the way that we also forgive our neighbor. Just as we daily sin much against God, and yet He forgives everything through grace, so we, too, must ever forgive our neighbor who does us injury, violence, and wrong, shows malice toward us, and so on. If, therefore, you do not forgive, then do not think that God forgives you (Matthew 18:23–25). But if you forgive, you have this comfort and assurance, that you are forgiven in heaven. This is not because of your forgiving. For God forgives freely and without condition, out of pure grace, because He has so promised, as the Gospel teaches. But God says this in order that He may establish forgiveness as our confirmation and assurance, as a sign alongside of the promise, which agrees with this prayer in Luke 6:37, "Forgive, and you will be forgiven." (LC III 93–96)

The Sixth Petition

This, then, is what "lead us not into temptation" means. It refers to times when God gives us power and strength to resist the temptation (1 Corinthians 10:13). However, the temptation is not taken away or removed. While we live in the flesh and have the devil around us, no one can escape his temptation and lures. It can only mean that we must endure trials—indeed, be engulfed in them (2 Timothy 2:3). But we say this prayer so that we may not fall and be drowned in them.

Therefore, we Christians must be armed (Ephesians 6:10–18) and daily expect to be constantly attacked. No one may go on in security and carelessly, as though the devil were far from us. At all times we must expect and block his blows. Though I am now chaste, patient, kind, and in firm faith, the devil will this very hour send such an arrow into my heart that I can scarcely stand. For he is an enemy that never stops or becomes tired. So when one temptation stops, there always arise others and fresh ones. (LC III 106, 109)

The Seventh Petition

You see again how God wishes for us to pray to Him also for all the things that affect our bodily interests, so that we seek and expect help nowhere else except in Him. But He has put this matter last. For if we are to be preserved and delivered from all evil, God's name must first be hallowed in us, His kingdom must be with us, and His will must be done. After that He will finally preserve us from sin and shame, and, besides, from everything that may hurt or harm us. (LC III 117–18)

166. How does praying for "daily bread" forge in your mind an attitude of dependence and thankfulness?

167. Describe how forgiveness in Christ is the motivation and strength for forgiving others.

168. How can God's people be instruments for providing "daily bread" to the world?

169. The Fifth Petition, Luther notes, serves to "[break] our pride and [keep] us humble" (LC III 90). Explain and apply this truth to your life.

170. What temptations do you—and all Christians—face today? How does the saying apply, "You cannot prevent birds from flying over your head, but you can certainly prevent them from building a nest in your hair"?

171. In what ways is the Lord's Prayer a model for your own prayers?

Partners in Prayer

Personal Reflection

- During the week, use one petition each day as a prayer theme (God's Name, Kingdom, Will, Daily Bread, Forgiveness, Temptation, Deliverance from Evil). Use the Introduction and Conclusion to frame your prayers.

- Join or explore the possibility of beginning a prayer ministry in your congregation. Start off small; invite new prayer partners to join in the months and year ahead.

- Think about the connection between each of the petitions of the Lord's Prayer. Look for ways to share God's blessings with others.

Family Connection

- As a family take turns identifying a blessing from God that begins with each letter of the alphabet.

- As a family study sections of the newspaper to identify examples of evil in the world. Thank God for the protecting care He continually provides.

- Ask each family member to give a metaphor for heaven (e.g., "Heaven is like . . ."). Talk about heaven as the place Jesus promises to all who love and trust in Him.

Closing Worship

Sing or read aloud these stanzas from "With the Lord Begin Your Task" (*LW* 483).

> With the Lord begin your task;
> Jesus will direct it.
> For His aid and counsel ask;
> Jesus will perfect it.
> Ev'ry morning with Jesus rise,
> And when day is ended,
> In His name then close your eyes;
> Be to Him commended.
>
> Let each day begin with prayer,
> Praise, and adoration.

On the Lord cast ev'ry care;
He is your salvation.
Morning, evening, and at night
Jesus will be near you,
Save you from the tempter's might,
With His presence cheer you.

For Next Week

Read Luther's questions and explanations on Holy Baptism.

Session 11

Baptized into Christ

The Sacrament of Holy Baptism

Law/Gospel Focus

Because of our rebellion and sin against God, human beings are separated from salvation and eternal life. Yet, in Christ, God has demonstrated His mercy and compassion toward all people. Baptism brings the Savior's work to us personally: baptized into His death and resurrection we are forgiven and given the blessings of life and salvation. In Baptism, God makes us His children and calls us together as the body of Christ.

Opening Worship

Read responsively the following litany based on Psalm 105.

Leader: Oh give thanks to the LORD, call upon His name; make known His deeds among the peoples!

Participants: **Sing to Him, sing praises to Him; tell of all His wondrous works!**

Leader: Glory in His holy name; let the hearts of those who seek the LORD rejoice!

Participants: **Seek the Lord and His strength; seek His presence continually.**

Water, Water Everywhere

Pharaoh's daughter bathed in it. The Roman emperor Augustus drank it. Napoleon trudged through it during his retreat from Waterloo. Visitors to London peer through it in the wintry gloom.

Water. We cannot live without it.

Scientists say that there is exactly the same amount of water on earth today as there has always been. The amount of water doesn't change, but its form does. Oceans and rivers, icebergs and ice cubes, mist and clouds—all are gifts of water.

For such an ordinary resource, water plays a remarkable role in life.

In his catechisms, Luther describes how God uses water and His Word in an extraordinary way.

172. When have you most appreciated water in your life?

173. In what ways do people take water for granted?

174. How does water connect us to creation? to one another?

Connected to the Word

The Small Catechism

The Sacrament of Holy Baptism

First

What is Baptism?

Baptism is not simple water only, but it is the water included in God's command and connected with God's Word.

Which is that Word of God?

Christ, our Lord, says in the last chapter of Matthew, "Go therefore and make disciples of all nations, baptizing them in the name of the Father and of the Son and of the Holy Spirit" (Matthew 28:19).

Second

What does Baptism give or profit?

It works forgiveness of sins, delivers from death and the devil, and gives eternal salvation to all who believe this, as the words and promises of God declare.

Which are these words and promises of God?

Christ, our Lord, says in the last chapter of Mark, "Whoever believes and is baptized will be saved, but whoever does not believe will be condemned" (Mark 16:16).

Third

How can water do such great things?

It is not the water indeed that does them, but the Word of God, which is in and with the water, and faith, which trusts this Word of God in the water. For without the Word of God the water is simple water and no Baptism. But with the Word of God it is a Baptism, that is, a gracious water of life and a washing of regeneration in the Holy Spirit. As St. Paul says in Titus chapter three, "He saved us . . . by the washing of regeneration and renewal of the Holy Spirit, whom He poured out on us richly through Jesus Christ our Savior, so that being justified by His grace we might become heirs according to the hope of eternal life. The saying is trustworthy" (vv. 5–8).

Fourth

What does such baptizing with water signify?

It signifies that the old Adam in us should, by daily contrition and repentance, be drowned and die with all sins and evil lusts. And also it shows that a new man should daily come forth and arise, who shall live before God in righteousness and purity forever.

Where is this written?

St. Paul says in Romans chapter 6, "We were buried therefore with Him by baptism into death, in order that, just as Christ was raised from the dead by the glory of the Father, we too might walk in newness of life" (Romans 6:4).

The Large Catechism

Let us not doubt that Baptism is divine. It is not made up or invented by people. For as surely as I can say, "No one has spun the Ten Commandments, the Creed, and the Lord's Prayer out of his head; they are revealed and given by God Himself." So also I can boast that Baptism is no human plaything, but it is instituted by God Himself. (LC IV 6)

To be baptized in God's name is to be baptized not by men, but by God Himself. Therefore, although it is performed by human hands, it is still truly God's own work. From this fact everyone may readily conclude that Baptism is a far higher work than any work performed by a man or a saint. For what work can we do that is greater than God's work? (LC IV 10)

Understand the difference, then. Baptism is quite a different thing from all other water. This is not because of its natural quality but because something more noble is added here. God Himself stakes His honor, His power, and His might on it. Therefore, Baptism is not only natural water, but a divine, heavenly, holy, and blessed water, and whatever other terms we can find to praise it. This is all because of the Word, which is a heavenly, holy Word, which no one can praise enough. For it has, and is able to do, all that God is and can do (Isaiah 55:10–11). (LC IV 17)

I encourage again that these two—the water and the Word—by no means be separated from each other and parted. For if the Word is separated from it, the water is the same as the water that the servant cooks with. It may indeed be called a bathkeeper's baptism. But when the Word is added, as God has ordained, it is a Sacrament. It is called Christ's Baptism. Let this be the first part about the holy Sacrament's essence and dignity.

In the second place, since we know now what Baptism is and how it is to be regarded, we must also learn why and for what purpose it is instituted. We must learn what it profits, gives, and works. For this also we cannot find a better resource than Christ's words quoted above, "Whoever believes and is baptized will be saved" (Mark 16:16). Therefore, state it most simply in this way: the power, work, profit, fruit, and purpose of Baptism is this—to save (1 Peter 3:21). For no one is baptized in order that he may become a prince, but, as the words say, that he "be saved." We know that to be saved is nothing other than to be delivered from sin, death, and the devil (Colossians 1:13–14). It means to enter into Christ's kingdom (John 3:5), and to live with Him forever. (LC IV 22–25)

In the third place, since we have learned Baptism's great benefit and power, let us see further who is the person that receives what Baptism gives and profits. This is again most beautifully and clearly expressed in the words "Whoever believes and is baptized will be saved" (Mark 16:16). That is, faith alone makes the person worthy to receive profitably the saving, divine water. Since these blessings are presented here and promised through the words in and with the water, they cannot be received in any other way than by believing them with the heart (Romans 10:9). (LC IV 32–33)

So you see plainly that there is no work done here by us, but a treasure, which God gives us and faith grasps (Ephesians 2:8–9). It is like the benefit of the Lord Jesus Christ upon the cross, which is not a work, but a treasure included in the Word. It is offered to us and received by faith. (LC IV 37)

Discussing the Texts

175. Who instituted Baptism? Why, according to Luther, is this institution so important?

176. How is Baptism *God's* work? How does God choose to administer Baptism?

177. What, at root, is Baptism's "power, work, profit, fruit, and purpose"?

178. How would you explain the following phrases:
works forgiveness of sins

rescues from death and the devil

gives eternal salvation

179. How are the water and the Word connected in Baptism? Why can the two *never* be separated?

180. How are faith and Baptism connected? How can the blessings of Baptism be refused?

181. Describe the "old Adam." What happens in Baptism?

182. Describe the "new man." What happens in Baptism?

183. How would you respond to the following statements:
"I decided to be baptized to show that I will follow Jesus."

"Babies have not had time to sin, so they do not need Baptism."

"Faith alone saves; I don't need to be baptized."

184. What does it mean to you that Baptism is not a work which we do, but is "a treasure included in the Word. It is offered to us and received by faith"?

A Lifelong Bath

God gives His blessings as a gift to all who are baptized into the triune name. Baptism signifies a state of being—the saving relationship into which God has given us rebirth through water and the Holy Spirit. Baptized into God's family, we are equipped with God's grace and strength to withstand the attacks of evil and to serve God in the new life He has given us.

The Large Catechism

Therefore, every Christian has enough in Baptism to learn and to do all his life. For he has always enough to do by believing firmly what Baptism promises and brings: victory over death and the devil (Romans 6:3–6), forgiveness of sin (Acts 2:38), God's grace (Titus 3:5–6), the entire Christ, and the Holy Spirit with His gifts (1 Corinthians 6:11). In short, Baptism is so far beyond us that if timid nature could realize this, it might well doubt whether it could be true. Think about it. Imagine there was a doctor somewhere who understood the art of saving people from death or, even though they died, could restore them quickly to life so that they would afterward live forever. Oh, how the world would pour in money like snow and rain. No one could find access to him because of the throng of the rich! But here in Baptism there is freely brought to everyone's door such a treasure and medicine that it utterly destroys death and preserves all people alive.

We must think this way about Baptism and make it profitable for ourselves. So when our sins and conscience oppress us, we strengthen ourselves and take comfort and say, "Nevertheless, I am baptized. And if I am baptized, it is promised to me that I shall be saved and have eternal life, both in soul and body." (LC IV 41–44)

185. What treasure have you received in Baptism? How does daily remembering your Baptism bring you to Christ?

186. In what ways does Baptism give us enough "to learn and to do" all our life?

187. How does Luther's illustration of the physician reveal the value of Baptism?

188. "I am baptized!" Describe the strength and comfort Baptism gives you in temptation and troubles.

189. How can you and your congregation celebrate Baptism in your life together?

Celebration of Regeneration

Personal Reflection

- If possible, talk with your parents and/or sponsors about your Baptism. Thank them for supporting and encouraging you in the faith into which you have been baptized.

- Videotape your congregation's Baptisms. (Get permission from your pastor!) Or take or obtain photographs of the newly baptized and display the pictures on a church bulletin board.

- Commemorate your baptismal birthday with a special donation of time, talent, or treasure in gratitude to God for the blessings of your Baptism.

Family Connection

- Have each family member show his or her baptismal certificate. Note the dates, times, places, sponsors, and pastor(s) involved in the service. Plan an annual remembrance and celebration for each Baptism.

- Send baptismal birthday cards to friends and extended family members after learning the dates on which they were baptized.

- Find ways to celebrate the relationship believers enjoy with one another as fellow members of God's family (e.g., invite someone without close family in the area to your home for meals and a time of togetherness).

Closing Worship

Sing or read aloud these stanzas from "Baptized into Your Name Most Holy" (*LW* 224).

Baptized into Your name most holy,
O Father, Son, and Holy Ghost,
I claim a place, though weak and lowly,
Among Your seed, Your chosen host.
Buried with Christ and dead to sin,
I have Your Spirit now within.

All that I am and love most dearly,
Receive it all, O Lord, from me.
Oh, let me make my vows sincerely,
And help me Your own child to be!
Let nothing that I am or own,
Serve any will but Yours alone.

For Next Week

Read Luther's questions and explanations on Confession and Absolution.

Session 12

Forgiveness—Personally Yours

Confession and Absolution

Law/Gospel Focus

All people are by nature alienated from God. We rebel against His Law; we have no will or strength to live according to His commandments. In Christ's death and resurrection, God reconciles us to Himself—fully and freely. He invites us to confess our sins and receive His forgiveness spoken through the Gospel, through pastors, and through our brothers and sisters in Christ.

Opening Worship

Read responsively the following litany based on Psalm 32.

Leader: Blessed is the one whose transgression is forgiven, whose sin is covered.

Participants: **Blessed is the man against whom the LORD counts no iniquity and in whose spirit there is no deceit.**

Leader: For when I kept silent, my bones wasted away through my groaning all day long.

Participants: **For day and night Your hand was heavy upon me; my strength was dried up as by the heat of summer.**

Leader: I acknowledged my sins to You, and I did not cover my iniquity.

Participants: **I said, "I will confess my transgressions to the LORD" and You forgave the iniquity of my sin.**

Leader: Therefore let everyone who is godly offer prayer to You at a time when You may be found; surely in the rush of great waters, they shall not reach him.

Participants: **You are a hiding place for me; You preserve me from trouble; You surround me with shouts of deliverance.**

A Good Word

"Gracious words are like a honeycomb, sweetness to the soul and health to the body" (Proverbs 16:24).

Words cheer. Words heal. At times, the best medicine for afflictions of body and soul is someone to talk to, someone with whom to share pleasant words.

In the catechisms, Luther describes the blessings of Confession and Absolution for God's people.

190. If you received good news today, whom would you tell first? Why?

191. If you received disturbing news today, whom would you tell first? Why?

192. In what ways is talking with a trusted, compassionate person a great blessing?

Forgiveness of Sins

The Small Catechism

How the Unlearned Should Be Taught to Confess

What is confession?

Confession has two parts: the one is that we confess our sins; the other is that we receive Absolution, or forgiveness, from the confessor, as from God Himself, and in no way doubt, but firmly believe that our sins are forgiven before God in heaven by this.

What sins should we confess?

Before God we should plead guilty of all sins, even of those that we do not know, as we do in the Lord's Prayer. But before the confessor we should confess only those sins that we know and feel in our hearts.

Which are these?

Here consider your calling according to the Ten Commandments, whether you are a father, mother, son, daughter, master, mistress, a manservant or maidservant. Consider whether you have been disobedient, unfaithful, or slothful. Consider whether you have grieved anyone by words or deeds, whether you have stolen, neglected, wasted, or done other harm.

What is the Office of the Keys?

The Office of the Keys is that special authority which Christ has given to His Church on earth to forgive the sins of repentant sinners, but to withhold forgiveness from the unrepentant as long as they do not repent.

Where is this written?

This is what St. John the Evangelist writes in chapter twenty: The Lord Jesus breathed on His disciples and said, "Receive the Holy Spirit. If you forgive anyone his sins, they are forgiven; if you do not forgive them, they are not forgiven." [John 20:22–23]

What do you believe according to these words?*

I believe that when the called ministers of Christ deal with us by His divine command, in particular when they exclude openly unrepentant sinners from the Christian congregation and absolve those who repent of their sins and want to do better, this is just as valid and certain, even in heaven, as if Christ our dear Lord dealt with us Himself.

* This question may not have been composed by Luther himself but reflects his teaching and was included in editions of the catechism during his lifetime.

The Large Catechism

In the first place, I have said that besides the Confession here being considered there are two other kinds, which may even more properly be called the Christians' common confession. They are (a) the confession and plea for forgiveness made to God alone and (b) the confession that is made to the neighbor alone. These two kinds of confession are included in the Lord's Prayer, in which we pray, "Forgive us our trespasses as we forgive those who trespass against us" (Matthew 6:12), and so on. In fact, the entire Lord's

Prayer is nothing else than such a confession. For what are our petitions other than a confession that we neither have nor do what we ought, as well as a plea for grace and a cheerful conscience? Confession of this sort should and must continue without letup as long as we live. For the Christian way essentially consists in acknowledging ourselves to be sinners and in praying for grace.

Similarly, the other of the two confessions, the one that every Christian makes to his neighbor, is also included in the Lord's Prayer. For here we mutually confess our guilt and our desire for forgiveness to one another (James 5:16) before coming before God and begging for His forgiveness (Matthew 5:23–24). Now, all of us are guilty of sinning against one another; therefore, we may and should publicly confess this before everyone without shrinking in one another's presence. (LC V: An Exhortation to Confession 8–10).

Besides this public, daily, and necessary confession, there is also the confidential confession that is only made before a single brother. If something particular weighs upon us or troubles us, something with which we keep torturing ourselves and can find no rest, and we do not find our faith to be strong enough to cope with it, then this private form of confession gives us the opportunity of laying the matter before some brother. We may receive counsel, comfort, and strength when and however often we wish. That we should do this is not included in any divine command, as are the other two kinds of confession. Rather, it is offered to everyone who may need it, as an opportunity to be used by him as his need requires. The origin and establishment of private Confession lies in the fact that Christ Himself placed His Absolution into the hands of His Christian people with the command that they should absolve one another of their sins (Ephesians 4:32). So any heart that feels its sinfulness and desires consolation has here a sure refuge when he hears God's Word and makes the discovery that God through a human being looses and absolves him from his sins.

So notice then, that Confession, as I have often said, consists of two parts. The first is my own work and action, when I lament my sins and desire comfort and refreshment for my soul. The other part is a work that God does when He declares me free of my sin through His Word placed in the mouth of a man. It is this splendid, noble, thing that makes Confession so lovely, so comforting. (LC V: An Exhortation to Confession 13–15).

Discussing the Texts

193. In his day, Luther lamented that Confession was compulsory. What abuses can and do occur in the Church with mandatory Confession?

194. What abuses can and do occur when Confession is voluntary?

195. What are the two parts of Confession? How does Luther describe each part in detail?

196. What, according to Luther, is essential to "the Christian way"? How does this summarize Confession?

197. Describe how the pastor speaks words "as from God Himself."

198. How does reflecting on the Ten Commandments drive us to Confession?

199. Explain the Office of the Keys. How does the Church carry on Christ's ministry in the Office of the Keys?

200. What kinds of sins should Christians confess to God?

201. What sins should we confess to pastors?

202. What sins should Christians confess to brothers and sisters in Christ?

Splendid, Precious, and Comforting

Baptized into the family of believers, each Christian enjoys full rights and privileges as children of God through faith in Christ Jesus. Among these privileges is that of being able to unburden our conscience and to receive the assurance that God in Christ has already removed from us the penalty of our sins.

The Large Catechism

In our view of Confession, therefore, we should sharply separate its two parts far from each other. We should place slight value on our part in it. But we should hold in high and great esteem God's Word in the Absolution part of Confession. We should not proceed as if we intended to perform and offer Him a splendid work, but simply to accept and receive something from Him. . . .

Moreover, no one may now pressure you with commandments. Rather, what we say is this: Whoever is a Christian or would like to be one is here faithfully advised to go and get the precious treasure. . . .

We strongly urge you . . . to make confession of your need, not with the intention of doing a worthy work by confessing but in order to hear what God has arranged for you to be told. What I am saying is that you are to concentrate on the Word, on the Absolution, to regard it as a great and precious and magnificently splendid treasure, and to accept it with all praise and thanksgiving to God.

So we teach what a splendid, precious, and comforting thing Confession is. Furthermore, we strongly urge people not to despise a blessing that in view of our great need is so priceless. . . .

When I urge you to go to Confession, I am doing nothing else than urging you to be a Christian (LC V: An Exhortation to Confession 18, 20, 22, 28, 32).

203. Because of Christ, we can "hold in high and great esteem God's Word," His Absolution. How does Jesus' death and resurrection help you openly to confess your sins?

204. *Absolution* is derived from the Latin "to set free." How does Confession and Absolution set you free with a "cheerful conscience"?

205. What do God's people accept and receive in Confession?

206. What does Luther urge the people of God to do with regard to Confession?

Make an Appointment

Personal Reflection

• If possible, make an appointment with your pastor for private Confession and Absolution.

• Consider your place in life according to the Ten Commandments: Are you a father, mother, son, daughter, husband, wife, or worker?

Have you been disobedient, unfaithful, or lazy? Have you been hottempered, rude, or quarrelsome? Have you hurt someone by your words or deeds? Have you stolen, been negligent, wasted anything, or done any harm? Confess these and all other sins to God. Then rejoice in the forgiveness Jesus earned for you on the cross.

- Find in a concordance a list of references describing God's forgiveness. Look up several of these and reflect on the blessing of God's forgiveness in your life.

Family Connection

- Find the "Confession" section in your hymnal or in a recent Sunday worship folder. Talk as a family about how each person can prepare for confession by reviewing the events in his or her life during the past week.

- Practice as a family confessing to one another and assuring one another of Jesus' full and complete forgiveness for all sins.

- As part of a family devotion have each family member write a sin on a small slip of paper. Then crumple these up and place them into the garbage. Talk about the complete removal of sins that Jesus provides.

Closing Worship

Sing or read aloud these stanzas from "Jesus Sinners Will Receive" (*LW* 229).

> Jesus sinners will receive;
> May they all this saying ponder
> Who in sin's delusions live
> And from God and heaven wander!
> Here is hope for all who grieve:
> Jesus sinners will receive.
>
> Come, O sinners, one and all,
> Come, accept His invitation;
> Come, obey His gracious call,
> Come and take His free salvation!
> Firmly in these words believe:
> Jesus sinners will receive.
>
> Jesus sinners will receive.
> Even me He has forgiven;

And when I this earth must leave,
I shall find an open heaven.
Dying, still to Him I cleave—
Jesus sinners will receive.

For Next Week

Read Luther's questions and explanations on the Sacrament of the Altar.

Session 13

Nourished in Christ

The Sacrament of the Altar

Law/Gospel Focus

Our fallen, sinful nature often leads us to discouragement, despair, and disobedience toward God's Word. Apart from God's love and strength, we are without hope—unable to save ourselves or continue in faith. In His body and blood, Christ gives His forgiveness, life, and salvation. As we eat and drink at His table, we are nourished for our life of faith and service.

Opening Worship

Read responsively the following litany based on Psalm 23.

Leader: The LORD is my shepherd, I shall not want.

Participants: **He makes me lie down in green pastures,**

Leader: He leads me beside still waters. He restores my soul.

Participants: **He leads me in paths of righteousness for His name's sake.**

Leader: Even though I walk through the valley of the shadow of death, I will fear no evil,

Participants: **For You are with me; Your rod and Your staff, they comfort me.**

Leader: You prepare a table before me in the presence of my enemies;

Participants: **You anoint my head with oil; my cup overflows.**

Leader: Surely goodness and mercy shall follow me all the days of my life,

Participants: **And I shall dwell in the house of the LORD forever.**

A Meal Together

"Sharing food with another human being is an intimate act that should not be indulged in lightly" (M. F. K. Fischer).

From ancient civilizations to the present, a meal together has served to forge a special bond between people. Whether at a banquet hall or home, eating and drinking becomes a celebration of friendship and unity.

In his catechisms, Luther describes God's rich blessings given in the Sacrament of the Altar.

207. What does the sharing of food signify in our world?

208. Tell about a meal together that was especially meaningful to you.

209. In what ways are we blessed—physically, emotionally, and socially—by eating together with family and friends?

No Ordinary Food

The Small Catechism

What is the Sacrament of the Altar?

Answer: It is the true body and blood of our Lord Jesus Christ, under the bread and wine, for us Christians to eat and to drink, instituted by Christ Himself.

Where is this written?

Answer: The holy Evangelists, Matthew, Mark, Luke, and St. Paul write:

Our Lord Jesus Christ, on the night He was betrayed, took bread, and when He had given thanks, He broke it and gave it to the disciples and said: "Take, eat; this is My body, which is given for you. This do in remembrance of Me."

In the same way also He took the cup after supper, and when He had given thanks, He gave it to them, saying, "Drink of it, all of you; this is My blood of the new testament, which is shed for you for the forgiveness of sins. This do, as often as you drink it, in remembrance of Me."

What is the benefit of such eating and drinking?

Answer: That is shown us in these words, "Given for you" and "shed for you for the forgiveness of sins." This means that in the Sacrament forgiveness of sins, life, and salvation are given us through these words. For where there is forgiveness of sins, there is also life and salvation.

How can bodily eating and drinking do such great things?

Answer: It is not the eating and drinking, indeed, that does them, but the words, which are given here, "Given . . . and shed for you, for the forgiveness of sins." These words are, beside the bodily eating and drinking, the chief thing in the Sacrament. The person who believes these words has what they say and express, namely, the forgiveness of sins.

Who, then, receives such Sacrament worthily?

Answer: Fasting and bodily preparation is, indeed, a fine outward training. But a person is truly worthy and well prepared who has faith in these words, "Given . . . and shed for you for the forgiveness of sins."

But anyone who does not believe these words, or doubts, is unworthy and unfit. For the words "for you" require hearts that truly believe.

The Large Catechism

It is the Word, I say, that makes and sets this Sacrament apart. So it is not mere bread and wine, but is, and is called, Christ's body and blood (1 Corinthians 11:23–27). For it is said, "When the Word is joined to the element or natural substance, it becomes a Sacrament." . . . The Word must make a Sacrament out of the element, or else it remains a mere element. Now, it is not the word or ordinance of a prince or emperor. But it is the Word of the grand Majesty, at whose feet all creatures should fall and affirm it is as

He says, and accept it with all reverence, fear, and humility (Isaiah 45:23; Philippians 2:10). (LC V 10–11)

Now examine further the effectiveness and benefits that really caused the Sacrament to be instituted. This is its most necessary part, so that we may know what we should seek and gain there. This is plain and clear from the words just mentioned, "This is My body and blood, given and shed *for you* for the forgiveness of sins." Briefly, that is like saying, "For this reason we go to the Sacrament: there we receive such a treasure by and in which we gain forgiveness of sins." "Why so?" "Because the words stand here and give us this. Therefore, Christ asks me to eat and drink, so that this treasure may be my own and may benefit me as a sure pledge and token. In fact, it is the very same treasure that is appointed for me against my sins, death, and every disaster." (LC V 20–22)

On this account it is indeed called a food of souls, which nourishes and strengthens the new man. For by Baptism we are first born anew (John 3:5). But, as we said before, there still remains the old vicious nature of flesh and blood in mankind. There are so many hindrances and temptations of the devil and of the world that we often become weary and faint, and sometimes we also stumble (Hebrews 12:3).

Therefore, the Sacrament is given as a daily pasture and sustenance, that faith may refresh and strengthen itself (Psalm 23:1–3) so that it will not fall back in such a battle, but become ever stronger and stronger. The new life must be guided so that it continually increases and progresses. But it must suffer much opposition. . . . Now to this purpose the comfort of the Sacrament is given when the heart feels that the burden is becoming too heavy, so that it may gain here new power and refreshment. (LC V 23–27)

Now we must also see who is the person that receives this power and benefit. That is answered briefly . . . : Whoever believes the words has what they declare and bring. For they are not spoken or proclaimed to stone and wood, but to those who hear them, to whom He says, "Take, eat," and so on. Because He offers and promises forgiveness of sin, it cannot be received except by faith. This faith He Himself demands in the Word when He says, "Given . . . and shed *for you* [emphasis added], " as if He said, "For this reason I give it, and ask you to eat and drink it, that you may claim it as yours and enjoy it." Whoever now accepts these words and believes that what they declare is true has forgive-ness. . . .

This is the entire Christian preparation for receiving this Sacrament worthily. Since this treasure is entirely presented in the words, it cannot be received and made ours in any other way than with the heart. (LC V 33–36)

Discussing the Texts

210. What, according to Luther, is the Sacrament of the Altar? How is it different from "mere" eating and drinking?

211. When and why was the Supper instituted? How is it connected to Good Friday?

212. "When the Word is joined to the external element or natural substance, it becomes a Sacrament." Explain.

213. Why is it difficult to confess and accept the Word of the Lord: "This is My body. . . . This is My blood"?

214. Why is the Supper appropriately called "a food of souls"?

215. What gifts does Christ give in the Supper?

216. Who receives the gifts of Christ in His Supper?

217. What preparation is necessary for receiving the Supper?

218. What causes Christians to neglect the Supper?

219. Why should Christians receive the Lord's Supper often?

Food for the Family

Special family gatherings generally involve favorite food, fellowship, and reminiscences. In the Lord's Supper members of the family of God receive Christ's body and blood in the bread and wine, commune together as we celebrate our oneness in the faith, and remember our Lord's life, death, and resurrection for the forgiveness of sins.

The Large Catechism

Here [in this Sacrament] He offers to us the entire treasure that He has brought for us from heaven. With the greatest kindness He invites us to receive it also in other places, like when He says in St. Matthew 11:28, "Come to Me, all who labor and are heavy laden, and I will give you rest." It is surely a sin and a shame that He so cordially and faithfully summons and encourages us to receive our highest and greatest good, yet we act so distantly toward it. We permit so long a time to pass without partaking of the Sacrament that we grow quite cold and hardened, so that we have no longing or love for it. We must never think of the Sacrament as something harmful from which we had better flee, but as a pure, wholesome, comforting remedy that grants salvation and comfort. It will cure you and give you life both in soul and body. For where the soul has recovered, the body also is relieved. (LC V 66–68)

But if you say, "What, then, shall I do if I cannot feel such distress or experience hunger and thirst for the Sacrament?" Answer, "For those who are of such a mind that they do not realize their condition I know no better counsel than that they put their hand into their shirt to check whether they have flesh and blood. (LC V 75)

220. In what ways has the Lord's Supper been meaningful to you in times of joy? in times of sadness and discouragement?

221. How would you respond to a believer who says the following: "My faith is weak. Should I go to Communion?"

"I'm ashamed of what I've done. Should I go to the Lord's Table?"

"I'm really feeling down this week. Does God want me to come to the Lord's Supper?"

222. Describe how the Supper benefits both soul and body.

223. In what ways is the Supper an expression of fellowship in your congregation? In what ways does it build fellowship?

224. How can we help baptized children to appreciate the Supper before they commune?

Christ Our Passover

Personal Reflection

• Read carefully the description of the Passover Meal (Exodus 12) and the description of the Lord's Supper (Luke 22). On a sheet of paper or in a journal, write down the similarities. Then write the ways that the Lord's Supper fulfills the focus and significance of the Passover.

- If possible, volunteer your time and effort to assist with the care of your congregation's altar and altar appointments.

- Review the words of the hymns under "The Lord's Supper." Look for God's promises to believers as we eat and drink the Lord's body and blood.

Family Connection

- Talk together about your participation in the Lord's Supper. If you have questions, plan to visit your pastor for a discussion.

- Sing your favorite hymns on the Lord's Supper. Share how the words both teach about and comfort believers with the meaning and significance of the Supper.

- Take a family "field trip" into your church sanctuary. As you approach the altar, talk about how congregation members come together to receive God's blessings in the Lord's Supper. Mention that we receive Christ's body and blood in the bread and wine consecrated on the altar because Jesus' one sacrifice took the place of the sacrifices Old Testament believers offered to God.

Closing Worship

Sing or read aloud these stanzas from "O Jesus, Blessed Lord, My Praise" (*LW* 245).

O Jesus, blessed Lord, my praise,
My heartfelt thanks to You I raise;
You have so lovingly bestowed
On me Your body and Your blood.

Break forth, my soul, in joy and say:
What wealth has come to you today,
What health of body, mind, and soul!
Christ dwells within me, makes me whole.